RACIAL CONSCIOUSNESS

This book is dedicated to Leo Kuper

Racial consciousness

Michael Banton

Professor of Sociology, University of Bristol

Longman
London and New York

Longman Group UK Limited,
Longman House, Burnt Mill, Harlow,
Essex CM20 2JE, England
and Associated Companies throughout the world.

Published in the United States of America
by Longman Inc., New York

First published 1988

British Library Cataloguing in Publication Data
Banton, Michael
    Racial consciousness
    1. Ethnicity
    I. Title
    305.8   GN495.6

    ISBN 0-582-02385-8   CSD
    ISBN 0-582-02384-X   PPR

Library of Congress Cataloging-in-Publication Data
Banton, Michael P.
    Racial consciousness/Michael Banton.
        p.   cm.
    Includes index.
    ISBN 0-582-02385-8.   ISBN 0-582-02384-X (pbk.)
    1. Race.   2. Race awareness.   3. Race relations.   I. Title.
    GN269.B36 1988   87-28595
    305.8--dc19   CIP

Set in AM Comp Edit 10/12 Baskerville

Produced by Longman Singapore Publishers (Pte) Ltd.
Printed in Singapore.

Contents

v

List of figures

List of tables

Acknowledgements

We are grateful to the following for permission to reproduce copyright material:

American Political Science Association for table 5.1 by Aberbach and Walker from American Political Science *Review*, Vol. 64 (1970); The Daily Telegraph plc for table 6.6 from a Gallup poll table in *The Daily Telegraph* (15.5.81); the author, Prof. M. Morner for tables 3.1 and 3.2 from *Race Mixture in the History of Latin America* (Little, Brown & Co. Inc.); Office of Population Censuses and Surveys for tables 6.1, 6.2, 6.3, 6.4 (*Labour Force Survey*, 1984) and fig. 1.2 (O.P.C.S. 1979); Policy Studies Institute for table 6.5 from PSI *Report* 646 by Brown and Gay; the author, Prof. M. Tumin for table 3.4 from *Social Class and Social Change in Puerto Rico* (Princeton University Press).

We are unable to trace the copyright owner of table 1.1 which appeared in the *Report*, Vol. 2 (1), May 1975 by the Federal Interagency Committee on Education and would appreciate any information which would enable us to do so.

CHAPTER 1
Physical and cultural differences

Anyone who takes a walk in a major British city will see people of a different skin colour, people whom he or she may classify as Asian, black, Chinese, Indian, white, etc. Some people may be difficult to classify. A person who reflects upon this will become aware of at least two things. Firstly, that there is a social process by which individuals are assigned to categories of this sort, even though there is often doubt about the best names for the categories and about the boundaries to be drawn between one category and another. Secondly, that people's consciousness of such differences varies according to circumstances. A person may not remember whether the bus-driver to whom he or she paid a fare two hours ago was black or white because colour does not signify very much in the relationship between a bus-driver and a passenger. But if that same person's sister had brought home a new boy-friend the previous week, he or she would remember whether the boy-friend was black or Asian or white, and a lot more about him, because a relationship that may lead to marriage has important consequences for the kinsfolk of the parties. To cite another example, the author remembers being invited to lunch at the home of a professor in California. He and his family prepared to say grace. The language was strange and the author thought to himself, 'It must be Hebrew. These people must be Jews!' Nothing had happened before then to make him perceive them as Jewish. Circumstances can also operate to make individuals classify themselves. Many a little girl must have come home from school and asked her mother why their home could not have a Christmas tree just like the homes of other children in her class. When her mother explained that Christmas trees were for Christians and that they did not have one because they were Jews (or Muslims) that may well have made the little girl

1

more conscious of being Jewish (or Muslim) than she was before.

The doubts about the correct name for a social category highlight certain features in the process of classification. Up to the 1970s, the British usually classified other people as either white or coloured. In recent years there has been some change in the use of the name 'coloured' and a tendency to replace it with 'black'. If people were to be divided into just two classes like this, the British were never sure whether they should consider dark-skinned Mediterrannean people as white or coloured. This was a doubt about where the boundary was to be drawn. Names reveal the criteria by which people are assigned and assign themselves to categories. Today white English people regularly refer to people from the Indian subcontinent as coloured and as Indians, just as they did in the 1950s, but now other possible names have been added such as the usually derogatory name 'Paki' and the more formal name of Asian to designate Indians, Pakistanis, Sri Lankans and others of ultimately South Asian origin. The people themselves may not mind being called Asians but prefer to be named by their religion (Hindu, Muslim, Sikh) or their national origin. To call them Asians is to classify them according to their geographical origin; to call them Indians is to classify them by their presumed national origin; to call them coloured is to classify them by their appearance. Some individuals are not easily classified. If, say, a girl has an Indian mother and an English father, is she to be assigned to the same category as her mother, her father or to a separate category, either of persons of mixed origin or of persons of intermediate appearance?

Just as it can be difficult to classify some individuals, so it can be difficult to decide by what criterion or criteria a group has been constituted. Jews are unquestionably a social group of some sort, but people dispute about whether they are a religious, a racial, an ethnic group, or some combination of all three. Something similar can be said about the English. Many white people in Britain distinguish between themselves as English and all other groups. They may accept that there are people appropriately named black British but question whether there are, or can be, black Englishmen and women. Yet if a mixed group of young men from London went to Glasgow to support a London football team they might well all count themselves and be considered English over against supporters of the Scottish side. Popular consciousness adapts to circumstances.

A study of a multiracial nursery school in Sweden found that the teachers grouped the children according to their home languages. All the Latin American children – Argentinian, Bolivian, Chilean,

2

Uruguayan, etc – went into one class and were referred to as 'the Spanish children'. There were five African children who all, unlike the Latin American children, spoke and understood Swedish well. They were placed in a Swedish-speaking class and referred to as Swedish children. The teachers knew that the Chilean children were not Spanish, and that the Nigerian children were not Swedish, but for the day-to-day running of the nursery that was less important than classification by language (Ehn 1986: 29–30). When, for convenience, larger ethnic categories are created in this way, people may not be conscious of their inaccuracies. A study of a town in north-west Ontario, Canada, found that there were residents often referred to as Ukrainians. This category included Poles, Romanians, Russians, and Yugoslavs. It was called Ukrainian because, apparently, Ukrainians were the most numerous of what appeared to others a category of relatively similar people. Finns gave their name to a Scandinavian category and Chinese to an East Asian category (see Fig. 1.1). The anthropologist who carried out this study (Stymeist 1975:50) heard someone in a bar addressed as 'Uke'. Instead of treating this name as simply a basis for interpersonal relations, as everyone else did, he asked the man if he was actually a Ukrainian. The answer was yes. The anthropologist then asked, in apparent innocence, 'What part of the Ukraine did your family come from?' and got the reply 'They didn't. They came from Poland, I'm a Polack.' He chose to present himself as Ukrainian because that was the local convention. The local people were not interested in what they saw as the finer details of differentiation in a faraway land. It is in this way that ethnic identities are redefined in a new situation.

PRACTICAL LANGUAGE

The classifications people use in everyday life are fashioned to that purpose and can be internally inconsistent without causing difficulties because people use the bit of the classificatory system that is appropriate to the circumstances and do not have to defend this system as a whole. Thus it is practical to group the children in the Swedish nursery according to their home languages. When men are joking with one another in a Canadian bar it is convenient to aggregate members of the smaller minorities into a regional group. However, anyone who has to compile a table of population statistics needs to work with a logically consistent scheme. Everyone must be

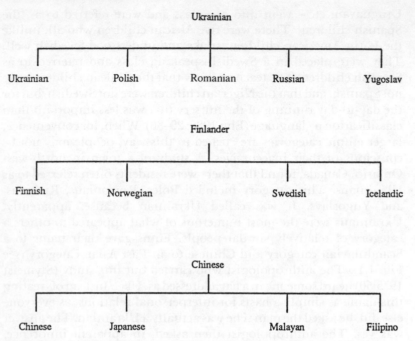

Figure 1.1 Ethnic categorization in an Ontario town

classified by country of birth, or country of father's birth, or by nationality, or by appearance, or by self-assignment. Practical considerations sometimes prevent the use of a fully consistent scheme, because such a scheme would be too large and complicated for many people to administer accurately. Consider the official United States classification in Table 1.1. Its criteria are a mixture of geographical origin and appearance. It refers to origins without specifying how these are to be measured. Many people have origins in more than one of the geographical regions. The fifth category is not properly consistent with the preceding ones. A person from Mexico may well have European origins and be considered white. Many people from Puerto Rico have African origins and are considered black. Many people classified as Caucasian because they were from the Indian subcontinent will not have been white; they were moved to the second category in 1977 when the classification was revised. The new scheme listed four racial and two ethnic categories but did not resolve the inconsistencies that stemmed from trying to base the categories on two kinds of criteria simultaneously (for further discussion see White 1979).

Table 1.1   Racial/ethnic categories authorized by United States federal government, 1975

1. *American Indian or Alaskan Native*: A person having origins in any of the original peoples of North America
2. *Asian or Pacific islander*: A person having origins in any of the original peoples of the Far East, South-east Asia, or the Pacific Islands. This area includes, for example, China, Japan, Korea, the Philippine Islands, and Samoa
3. *Black/negro*: A person having origins in any of the black racial groups of Africa
4. *Caucasian/white*: A person having origins in any of the original peoples of Europe, North Africa, the Middle East, or the Indian subcontinent
5. *Hispanic*: A person of Mexican, Puerto Rican, Cuban, Central or South American, or other Spanish culture or origin, regardless of race

(*Source: Federal Interagency Committee on Education Report*, vol. 2(1), May 1975)

These examples show that it can be useful to distinguish between folk concepts and analytical (or scientific) concepts. People in the United States think they know who is black and who is white. They call this a racial classification. They operate with a folk concept of race which has no scientific validity. Classification surfaced as a political problem in Britain when the government decided that there should be a question in the 1981 census to gather up-to-date information about the number of people belonging to racial and ethnic minorities. Pilot surveys were constructed to discover the most suitable wording for such a question. A sample of one such question is reproduced in Fig. 1.2. It was tried out in Haringay, north London, in 1979. Heads of households were asked, on a voluntary basis, to answer for all members of the household. Whereas in surveys of this kind normally 70 per cent of people co-operate, in this instance only 14 per cent of West Indian and 34 per cent of Asian households completed their forms. There was resistance to the whole inquiry, partly because of suspicions about the government's intentions, but also in some measure because of objections to the wording of the questions. The government then ordered that the census should go ahead without this question. People have their own ideas about what they consider the most appropriate names for themselves and others like them.

The doubts about what are the best names for groups, and where the boundaries are to be drawn, show that the groups people recognize in everyday life are multidimensional. The English constitute a recognizable group in respect of nationality, religion,

Racial consciousness

11 Parents' country of birth

Write the country of birth of:

(a) the person's father;

(b) the person's mother.

This question should be answered even if the person's father or mother is no longer alive. (If country not known, write 'NOT KNOWN'.)

Give the name by which the country is known today.

(a) Father born in (country)

....

(b) Mother born in (country)

....

---

11 Racial or ethnic group

Please tick the appropriate box to show the racial or ethnic group to which the person belongs

If the person was born in the United Kingdom of West Indian, African, Asian, Arab, Chinese, or 'Other European' descent, please tick one of the boxes numbered 2 to 10 to show the group from which the person is descended

1 ☐ English, Welsh, Scottish, or Irish

2 ☐ Other European

3 ☐ West Indian or Guyanese

4 ☐ African

5 ☐ Indian

6 ☐ Pakistani

7 ☐ Bangladeshi

8 ☐ Arab

9 ☐ Chinese

10 ☐ Any **other** racial or ethnic group, or if of **mixed** racial or ethnic descent (please describe below)

....

Figure 1.2 Question on race and ethnicity drafted for British census of 1981
(*Source*: OPCS *Test Census Schedule for Private Households, 1979*)

language and culture, but the distinctions between them and other groups are not clear cut. The English share United Kingdom citizenship with the Scots, Welsh and Northern Irish and this tends to obscure their nationality; they are not all members of the Church of England; their pronunciation may be distinctive but they share their language with others in North America, Australia, New Zealand, South Africa, etc. Minority groups in Britain are distinctive on several dimensions also, chiefly appearance but sometimes religion, language and culture as well. Another way of representing this

6

variability is to see group boundaries as a series of circles. Sometimes these coincide so that two boundaries are congruent; for example a circle round the Sikhs as an ethnic group would be the same as one round Sikhs as a religious group. Sometimes the circles overlap. Thus nearly all Bangladeshis are Muslims, but the category 'Muslim' includes people from other national and ethnic groups as well. A circle round the people who speak 'BBC English' would overlap one round individuals classed as 'Church of England', and most of it would come inside a circle delimiting people of English nationality. Any particular set of individuals is likely to consist of people who share attributes with many but not all members of the set. Folk classifications reflect the expectation that English people will be of 'white' appearance, have grown up in England, will speak in a particular way, profess Christianity and so on. Folk classifications change. From the Middle Ages up to the eighteenth century Europeans thought of themselves very much in religious terms and differentiated themselves from people of other faiths. In the nineteenth century, first national and then racial classification came to the fore.

It was for reasons such as these that Everett and Helen Hughes (1952: 131) once observed 'a considerable part of Sociology consists of cleaning up the language in which common people talk of social and moral problems'. The discussion has already hinted at three steps necessary for cleaning up the language. Firstly, it is vital to recognize that physical differences do not of themselves give rise to cultural differences. There are intermediate variables which parallel those which transform sex into gender. The biological differences between males and females are utilized as justifications for customary expectations about the kinds of behaviour considered appropriate. Expectations of gender roles are culturally constructed and maintained. They vary from one society to another and they change over time. Inferences about whether another person is male or female may be important as guides to the correct way of behaving towards him or her. Gender relations and racial relations can both be analysed in terms of role expectations. Physical appearance (or phenotype, to use the technical term), costume and names can all be role signs. People think 'because she has a dark skin she may be a West African', or 'because he wears a turban he's almost certainly a Sikh', just as they think 'because he wears a clerical collar of that kind he's presumably a Catholic priest', or 'because her name is Cohen she must be Jewish'. Behind these inferences is the assumption that people differ in important ways and should be treated accordingly, though there is

7

much variation because the signs are not always read in the same ways and beliefs about the special characteristics of West Africans, Sikhs, Catholic priests, and Jews may be quite wrong. When a word that describes a physical difference is also used to designate a social category it may distract attention from the process by which physical features are given social meaning.

Social differences are often taken for granted when they seem to have a physical basis. In the 1960s a political movement among Afro-Americans succeeded in forcing white Americans to reconsider their ideas about black people and their claims as citizens. An important element in the campaign was the rejection of the adjective 'coloured' and the promotion of black consciousness. This is discussed in greater detail in Chapter 5, but at this point it is useful to note that the black strategy was copied by women's groups which have concentrated upon 'consciousness raising'. They have sought to make women more aware of the ways in which sexual difference has been used to rationalize expectations. Their activity draws attention to a point of general application. Role signs indicate the behaviour expected in particular situations and there may be dispute or struggle about whether a distinction recognized in one situation is relevant in another. Names and titles are signals of expectations. In West European languages it has been customary for the last two centuries or so to employ different titles for married and unmarried women while making no corresponding distinction for men. Women have recently objected to a difference in titles in circumstances in which marital status is irrelevant, and so they have sought to introduce another female title that could be used for both the married and the unmarried. For some the use of the new title has been a point of principle. It was a sign of how they saw themselves and of how they wished others to see them. Designations of racial groups can have a similar significance.

Secondly, if ordinary language is to be 'cleaned up' it is essential to appreciate that the word 'race' in its application to humans has several meanings. These are discussed in Chapter 2, but one caution must be entered immediately. No one has ever seen another person's race. People perceive phenotypical differences of colour, hair form, underlying bone structure, and so on. For historical reasons, phenotypical variations came to be the basis for what, in Western European culture in particular circumstances, were called racial classifications. They could have been called something else. There are therefore three levels of abstraction. On the first, people perceive physical differences. On the second level they use these perceptions as signs of expected behaviour. There may then be a third level in which they describe their ideas about who belongs where as a racial classification. The first and second levels are common to most societies. The third is limited to a particular culture, though it has since been exported and adopted in other cultural regions thereby occasioning confusion and misunderstanding. 'Race' is often used as if it were an objective, scientific, and culture-free designation of differences of appearance. It is not. The very use of this word to identify such a kind of classification brings with it a host of cultural associations deriving from the historical circumstances in which the word acquired a special meaning. For the purposes of scientific classification a better set of terms is available.

Thirdly, it is as well to remember that classifications and definitions which are suitable for one purpose may not be so suitable for another. Folk classifications of people's 'race' vary from place to place and are adapted to the requirements of everyday life. People are usually conscious that they themselves belong somewhere in such a classification and think of others as having their places in it. An analytical or scientific classification seeks to classify humans by principles that are unaffected by popular consciousness. A person belongs in a particular blood group whether or not he knows about it. A person's complexion may, to the specialist, be an indicator that the person is more likely to have a particular gene, just as being male is an indicator that the person is more likely to be colour-blind, but these are statistical associations which have no implications for the way people should behave towards each other. Only with the progress of biological science in the twentieth century has this been properly appreciated. Those responsible for health care can now benefit from studies showing the frequency with which certain genes occur in the racial minorities by comparison with the majority population, but this bears very little relation indeed to any folk classification.

Racial consciousness is not easily defined because it is a distillation of personal experience. In one form it is an individual's interpretation of how his or her life is affected by the way others assign him or her to a racial category. In another form, it is an individual's tendency to assign others to racial categories. While racial consciousness varies from one person to another, there are also common elements. If those who are assigned to a particular category are treated similarly they are likely to share this experience. They also project their own experience when they respond to information about other countries. Men can experience a common bond with men in a different society; women with women; whites with whites, and blacks

9

with blacks. If it were possible to clean up the language thoroughly, then the adjective 'racial' would be discarded. Groups could be identified as Asian, black, Jewish, white, or by whatever names were in everyday use. Since this is not possible, at least at present, the adjective 'racial' is here applied to any classification based on physical appearance and is not restricted to classifications influenced by nineteenth-century theories of racial superiority and inferiority.

Every academic subject, and every profession, seeks greater precision in the use of words, but there is one field which should be of particular help to sociologists of racial relations. This is that branch of law that relates to the prohibition of racial discrimination. Courts of law have to be consistent in the way they define terms and how they apply them to behaviour because so much depends upon the result. There is substantial agreement internationally about the definition of racial discrimination and a growing agreement about related concepts like prejudice and incitement to racial hatred.

RACIAL RELATIONS

The Parliament of the United Kingdom in 1965, 1968, and 1976 agreed to legislation which it called Race Relations Acts. They prohibit discrimination between persons 'on racial grounds'. Unlawful discrimination was initially defined in terms of the intention of the discriminator. On this point the law is in harmony with popular consciousness. It enables a court to base its judgment upon what ordinary people assume to be racial groups and it does not have to ask a scientist whether the popular ideas are scientifically correct. Ordinary people assume that 'race relations' are inter-racial relations and that these in some way constitute a special kind of relations that can be distinguished from intra-racial relations. The law does not need to define race relations. Parliament called them Race Relations Acts because members of the public were accustomed to thinking of relations between white people and people of another colour as race relations, and Parliament wanted to stop the discrimination which arose from, or was justified by, such ways of thinking. In so doing, Parliament reinforced the idea that relations between people of different physical appearance are in some way distinctive. It would have been less confusing had they been called Prevention of Discrimination Acts.

Official action will be the more effective if social scientists can improve the general understanding of why inter-racial relations differ from intra-racial relations. The sociologist, in particular, should be able to compare inter-racial relations with other kinds of intergroup relations, like inter-ethnic, inter-religious, inter-linguistic group relations, to find the causes of the difference. (Since ethnic, religious, and linguistic are adjectives it is only consistent to use the adjectival form 'racial' when using it to differentiate one kind of social relations.) The sociologist has to contend with the initial difficulty of defining a racial relation. There is a folk concept of racial relations, to be sure, but it seems too vague to be of use for analytical purposes. If one man invites another out for a drink and they are both of the same colour, that is presumably a relationship of friendship, not of race. If they are of different colour does that make it a racial relation? Unless a clear answer can be given to this question it is impossible to start examining what makes inter-racial relations different.

To begin with it is important to appreciate that interpersonal relations are many-stranded. When two people meet they can interact with one another on the basis of different relationships or they can change from one to another. Two students could interact on the basis of the same or different gender, the same or different generation, the same or different religion, as students of the same or different subjects, supporters of the same or different sporting teams, and so on. There is a social relation between them because they are interacting with one another, behaving in ways that respond to one another. The way they behave at any particular time depends upon how they negotiate the relevant relationship. For example, a female student might ask a male student for advice about something connected with her studies, in terms of the relationship between fellow students. He might attempt to change it into a male–female relationship. She might either agree to interact on this basis or decline to do so. To describe things in this way is to draw a distinction between a relation (between individuals) and a relationship (between roles).

What the law calls race relations are therefore, in a strict sense, racial relationships. They are interactions in which the behaviour of one or both parties is influenced by a belief that it is appropriate to behave differently when the parties are not of the same race. For a person to discriminate racially it is not necessary that he or she should be racially conscious in the sense that he or she could say, 'I know that man was of a different race and therefore I treated him differently.' It may be that the person in question had little insight into his or her motives, or was simply confused, but others could see that he or she treated people of a different race in a different way. It is also possible for someone to be mistaken in thinking that another is of the same or different race. Inferences are made from people's names and from accents heard over the telephone. There is a medical condition known as Nelson's disease in which the skin of 'white' people turns brown, and they become the victims of racial discrimination; they are not of different race if this is defined in terms of their genetic inheritance, but they are if race is defined by reference to differential treatment.

If social relations are many-stranded, race may be one of the strands. A relation between a white person and a black person is not necessarily a racial relation. It becomes one only when one of them treats the other differently on racial grounds. Differential treatment may constitute discrimination in the legal sense but does not necessarily do so. The law has been drafted to protect people from being treated unfavourably in employment, education, the provision of goods, facilities, and services (like housing), and the disposal or management of premises. It deals with situations in which one party can grant or withhold something of material value. There are many everyday encounters which entail no more than the granting or withholding of friendship and courtesy; these are not covered by the law, though victims of discrimination are sometimes awarded sums of money by the courts in recognition of the hurt to their feelings. A sociological approach must be broader than that of the law. Any kind of difference in behaviour associated with an assumed difference in physical appearance or ancestry can be racially motivated. Whenever such motivation can be inferred, then there are racial relationships.

A person who is accused of racial discrimination may be quick to protest that he or she has been involved in a many-stranded relation, and that it was some other strand, not a racial one, that caused him or her to behave in a particular way. But for the most part the general public is not bothered about such niceties. Their attention is caught more by reports of bad relations, tension, conflict, injustice, etc. What are good racial relations? Can there be any such relations? After all might it not be said that the ideal would be for people to pay no attention to differences of colour? Or to pay no more attention to skin colour than to eye colour? In such circumstances there would be no racial relations at all. Without going this far, there is implicit in the way most people approach any general discussion of these matters an idea of a scale, with the 'bad' at the one end and the 'good' ones at the other. Sociologists should not study only the 'bad' cases. They should be able to explain why the cases are at one point in the scale rather than another. Their analyses should provide guidance about the kind of action that would make it possible for a society to move nearer to the 'good' end of the scale. It is therefore important to define that end. This is difficult because the scale is based on 'bad' things like discrimination, riots, expressions of hatred, and so on. The 'good' end marks an absence of these things and it is difficult to find a word that suggests a possible quality. The least unsatisfactory is 'harmony'. It is unsatisfactory because highly unequal relations have often appeared harmonious. Slaves have appeared contented, and systems based upon slavery have persisted for centuries. A more positive word to define the good end of the scale would be 'justice', but this introduces other problems. Philosophers have been trying to define justice for over 2,000 years and it is still a subject for lively debate. People appeal to justice as an ideal or a standard by which to judge prevailing circumstances. It is something outside and independent of those circumstances. Sociologists need to compare different sets of social relations. They may call one set harmonious if there are no signs of friction. At the same time they may conclude that appearances are deceptive and point to other signs which lead them to expect changes; or they may reach a private judgement that the circumstances are unfair to one section of the population. So the notion of harmony is not a simple one.

CONFLICT

It is scarcely any easier to define the 'bad' end of the scale. One solution would be to call the bad end 'conflict', since there is a folk concept of conflict as a fight or a struggle. The scale would then become a scale of harmony and conflict. The objection to such a solution is that conflict is not necessarily bad. There are both constructive and destructive conflicts. Consider conflict between trade unions and employers. Worker pressure upon management (including strikes and the threat of strikes) sometimes forces firms to be more efficient and more productive. Conflict is then constructive. It is also possible that a prolonged strike could lead to the destruction of an industry, the market for the product being captured by producers in another country. Such conflict would be destructive. The difference between the two kinds of conflict can be represented by borrowing expressions from the language used in the theory of games.

Imagine a game between two players. If the gains and losses of the two players are added up at the end, and the total is more than zero, that is a positive-sum outcome. If the total is less than zero that is a negative-sum outcome. The third possibility is a zero-sum outcome. If there is a conflict between employees and an employer, and when the net gains and losses of the two parties are added up they come to a positive figure, that may be considered a constructive conflict. It could be that increased wages quickly compensate the employees for any loss of earnings during a strike so that they benefit, or that new rates of payment result in higher output so the employer benefits, or that both benefit. Provided the total benefit exceeds the losses, the conflict has been constructive. If the total losses are greater than the total gains, the conflict has been destructive. Many contests are of a zero-sum character in which one party can gain only at the other's expense and the total is therefore zero.

Parties to a conflict can never be sure whether they will make a net gain or a net loss, or whether the overall outcome will be positive, negative or zero. One party might initiate a conflict knowing there to be a risk that in the short run it might lose, but believing that in the long run not only would it gain but that the outcome would be to the general good (after all, parties to any struggle often claim that the interests of their group coincide with the interests of society!). The sociologist uses the word 'conflict' to identify the signs of struggle, but without making any assumption about the results to which it will lead. Yet if conflict can lead to harmony that implies that conflict should not be seen as the end point of a scale but as a position in a kind of spiral. This is discussed, with examples, in Chapter 4.

Most human behaviour can be understood only if it is seen as behaviour governed by rules. There are rules which govern fights and struggles. Football teams struggle with one another according to rules. Players and clubs which break the rules can be suspended. Strikers and their employers are engaged in a struggle, but the state lays down rules about how it may be conducted. States go to war with one another, but there are said to be rules of warfare and international conventions about such matters as the treatment of prisoners. Only in extreme circumstances do people recognize no restraints whatever. It can therefore be important to distinguish the extent to which a struggle is regulated by rules. Ordinary language recognizes a difference between competition and conflict. Football teams are engaged in competition because the area of struggle is limited to a short period, in special circumstances, and closely regulated. When the final whistle is blown the struggle may cease. The word 'conflict' is applied to struggles which endure longer, affect a bigger part of the participants' lives, and are less closely regulated. Some conflicts are between two sections of a society with both sides appealing to values shared by most members of that society. It is often said that the outcome of some industrial disputes depends upon which side gets the support of the public. These are conflicts within societies and they have to be distinguished from conflicts which split societies and result in partition. When a deep fissure is opening up and one side is demanding that it be recognized as an independent state, it may be more appropriate to speak of a cleavage than a conflict. Competition, conflict, and cleavage are names for different degrees of struggle. At present it is not possible to define conflict in such a way that it can be used as part of a set of analytic concepts. It is better to stay with the loose popular sense of the word and to concentrate upon understanding the facts about the interaction of peoples.

Popular ideas about racial relations reflect individual experiences and the images generated by the mass media. They do not provide a reliable basis for the understanding of what gives those relations their character, any more than the experience of the shopper in the supermarket enables him or her to understand the working of the economy. To understand racial relations it is necessary to look beyond popular consciousness to the social structures that give it form. This is not a one-way relationship, for popular ideas also influence structures, and the two interact in ways that are related to the society's environment. Two racially distinctive groups whose members encounter one another in equal relationships will interpret their experiences differently from people who meet only as superordinates and subordinates (as is usually the case in South Africa, for example). How they interpret that experience may also be influenced by prevailing beliefs about the results of scientific research into physical differences. Those beliefs usually over-simplify and distort scientific findings. Since the sociologist hopes to communicate with people other than fellow sociologists, he or she has to start from the popular assumption that certain kinds of social relations are racial relations and then go on to correct the errors that flow from popular understandings.

CHAPTER 2

Accounting for differences

'What is race?' seems a simple question, and those who ask it often think there must be a simple answer. Some of them make the mistake of assuming that because there is a word there must be something in the natural world that corresponds with that word. This is a philosophical error. There is also a historical dimension, because the word 'race' is less than 500 years old. There have been physical differences between humans for thousands of years, but it is only within the last two centuries that these differences have been conceptualized as racial. The use of ideas of race to organize evidence about human variation has entered the popular consciousness and influenced relations between groups. To unravel its social significance it is best to proceed historically, showing how and why the word 'race' has acquired additional meanings.

One of the earliest uses of 'race' to designate a set of people is to be seen in the reference to 'the race and stocke of Abraham' in Foxe's *Book of Martyrs* of 1570. The set of people so designated were Abraham's lineage. The word has continued to be used in this sense down to the present time. Looking back from the vantage-point of a later generation it can be seen that this first sense contained an ambiguity. It designated a set of people who were (a) of common descent, and (b) similar in significant respects. They were similar because they were of common descent. Yet two humans (or two animals or two plants) could be of common descent yet dissimilar, or of different descent but similar. If race was to be used as a name for a class of individuals that class had to be based on either descent or similarity of appearance. The ambiguity can be demonstrated by reference to a prominent descendant of Abraham's, Moses. According to the Old Testament (Exodus 2: 15; Numbers 12: 1), Moses was a

Levite who married a Midianite woman, Zipporah, who bore him two sons, Gershom and Eliezer. Later he married an Ethiopian woman (who may have been black, since his brother and sister 'spoke against him' for doing so – though, of course, they may have disliked his marrying a Midianite, too). If the second wife had borne him a son, he would have been of 'the race and stocke' of Levi just like his father and half-brother. To say this would be to use race in the sense of lineage. Yet if some contemporary anthropologist had set out to classify the individuals taking appearance as the criterion of race, Moses, Gershom, and Eliezer would have been accounted Semites, the second wife an Ethiopian, and Moses' third son a hybrid.

Scientific understanding of the nature of variation was assisted in the eighteenth century by the much improved scheme of classification formulated by the Swedish natural historian Linnaeus. This scheme was based on the outward appearance of the specimens to be classified, including observations about growth and habitat. The natural world was divided into three kingdoms: animal, vegetable, and mineral. Within the animal kingdom, creatures were classified in orders, humans being asssigned to the Primates. Within this then came a number of smaller classes: family, genus, species, variety. The criterion of species was fertility and the example often cited was that of the mule. If a horse is mated with a donkey the offspring is a mule. A mule is infertile. By this criterion the horse and the donkey were considered separate species. A variety is a subdivision of a species; its members can mate with those assigned to other varieties of the same species and produce fertile offspring. So if Moses had a third son and there were other males and females resulting from crosses between Israelites and Ethiopians, they would have constituted a variety. They might indeed have been called a race. To call them such would be to use the word for a class of specimens of similar appearance irrespective of descent. Moses' third son would have been assigned to a different race if the criterion were similarity instead of descent.

The growth of scientific knowledge was, of course, influenced by the ideas that prevailed in the societies to which natural historians and philosophers belonged. By far and away the most powerful of these influences were those that stemmed from religious faith, and particularly from the belief that the Old Testament provided a straightforward account of the creation of the world some 6,000 years earlier. It declared that all humans descended from Adam and Eve. The Old Testament appeared to account for differences by providing genealogies showing how, by descent, people acquired membership in groups. Eighteenth century classifications of humans harmonized

17

the more easily with such an outlook because of the ambiguity in the idea of race as lineage. In that century political influences exerted scarcely any influence upon the scientific understanding of race despite the agitation over the slave-trade in the 1780s and 1790s. The debate about that trade was conducted within a framework of knowledge which presumed Africans to be inferior because they lived in an unhealthy climate and lacked the kinds of political and social institutions which encouraged economic development. For the abolitionists, the central issues were the doubtful morality and necessity of the trade. Only a handful of pro-slavery writers asserted that blacks were permanently inferior; most pro-slavery writers rejected such views except in so far as they contended that only Negroes could work in extreme heat. The slave-traders had no doubt about the humanity of those whose bodies they bought. The anti-Negro opinions of one pro-slavery writer, Edward Long, are sometimes quoted as if he were representative of a large body of white opinion. Long was also a sharp critic of colonial government and of West Indian slavery, so it was the abolitionist leader William Wilberforce who in Parliament frequently cited Long as the great authority on slavery, and not the pro-slavery side. If Long's arguments are to be interpreted as an ideology advancing material interests, they were not the interests of the slave-owners.

The ambiguity in the sense of race as lineage reflected the difference between a historical view of connections over time and a classificatory approach starting from differences in the present. The confusion increased at the beginning of the nineteenth century when the great French anatomist Cuvier introduced his concept of type. At this time the three lowest classes in the classificatory scheme were those of genus, species, and variety. To use words like 'race' and 'type' for purposes of classification was confusing. Were they additional to genus, species, and variety? Or substitutes? If substitutes, for which terms did they substitute? The problem arose because it was so difficult to separate the question of classification from beliefs about the historical dimension.

EXPLANATIONS

When, in the early nineteenth century, men asked why the peoples of the world were of varied appearance, they could turn to four possible answers. The first was divine intervention. It was suggested that, being descended from Adam and Eve, everyone had been of similar appearance until God placed a curse upon the descendants of Ham and made them black. God had apparently at some stage chosen to give other peoples yellow, brown, and reddish complexions. The second answer was that of climate: the sun had burned some peoples black. The difficulty, though, was that while Europeans could become sunburned this condition was not passed to a father's or mother's children. There was no inheritance of acquired characters. The third answer was the one now known to be correct: that variations arising accidentally in the course of conception had been selectively preserved. Until Darwin assembled evidence in favour of the theory of natural selection this explanation seemed both improbable and contrary to Scripture. So there was support for a fourth kind of answer. This was the theory that the world was divided into a series of natural provinces. Thus it was only in Australia that kangaroos and other marsupials were found. Likewise only there were Australian Aborigines resident: they corresponded to the marsupials in being the sorts of human suited to that environment. They were one out of a finite number of permanent racial types which had existed without change for a very long period, perhaps since the creation of the earth, or perhaps since some great catastrophe like Noah's flood or a series of volcanic eruptions, had upset the pattern. This doctrine is sometimes called catastrophism. It expounded an anti-evolutionary, steady-state view of the universe, and in its application to humans is called racial typology.

Racial typology presented the main kinds of humans as distinct species rather than varieties, despite all the evidence that sexual unions between them produced fertile offspring. It taught that each type was superior in its own province and that it was futile for humans to emigrate to provinces for which nature had not intended them. Europeans would never succeed in permanently colonizing North America. Since humans did not properly understand the conditions governing their lives, they mated with people of different type and races became mixed; but nature set limits to such deviation so that the pure types were permanent and unchanging. None of the proponents of racial typology held strictly to the logic of their doctrine. To some of them it seemed obvious that the whites were taking over other regions, demonstrating a greater capacity to develop them, and were therefore a superior race. The 1850s have been identified as the decade in which theories of 'scientific racism' were first advanced.

There was nothing remarkable about belief in racial superiority in

19

the eighteenth and early nineteenth centuries. Europeans were obviously superior to Africans in the ships they built, their navigational instruments, their development of writing, and so on, but this superiority was attributed to the methods of social and political organization they had developed in what was thought to be a congenial and stimulating environment. Africans and other backward peoples would be able to catch up in a few generations. The new doctrines of the mid-nineteenth century were very different. They fostered the beliefs that whites were *permanently* superior to blacks and that the two groups were not two varieties of a common species but two species of a common genus. They encouraged anthropologists to concentrate upon measuring human heads on the supposition that differences in the capacity for civilization were the result of differences in brain size. Typology was a new mode of accounting for observable differences and one which could easily be understood by non-specialists. It popularized a new concept of race as type which was to acquire fateful significance in the Nazis' doctrine of race. It presented blacks, whites, and yellows as different species (just as lions, tigers, leopards, and jaguars are different species within the genus *Panthera*) and it suggested that social relations between human types had to be different on account of these zoological distinctions. It has not yet been eliminated from the popular consciousness though it is much less influential than it once was. Nevertheless, it is important when reading historical material not to project this idea backwards in time. When writers in the seventeenth, eighteenth, and early ninetenth centuries used the word 'race', they did not mean by it what the racial typologists meant.

Two leading racial typologists were the Scottish anatomist Robert Knox who published *The Races of Men* in 1850 and the French Count Arthur de Gobineau who published his four-volume *Essay on the Inequality of Human Races* in 1853–54. Both men regarded the revolutionary movements in Europe in 1848 as the expression of racial forces. Neither provided any justification of European expansion overseas; indeed Knox was vehemently critical of imperialism. In the United States the leading exposition of typology was *Types of Mankind* by J. C. Nott and G. R. Gliddon, published in 1854. *Types of Mankind* was not welcomed by the defenders of slavery in that country, most of whom relied upon the Bible as a sufficient support for their views and rejected any suggestion that Negroes were not, like themselves, descended from Adam and Eve. With the increasing political power of the white, non-slave-holding working class before and after the Civil War, that changed, and doctrines of permanent black inferiority gained widespread acceptance among whites. In Britain the expression of racial prejudice seems to have become more common after about 1870, partly because of increased social mobility. One way in which people could advance their own status was by disparaging other people; and a dark colour was a definite social disadvantage. Imperialist policies were particularly unpopular in the 1860s; they began to gain support only after 1874 and then for reasons unconnected with racial doctrines. It does appear that beliefs in white superiority gained a strong grasp upon popular consciousness in the closing years of the nineteenth century, but the nature of the change in opinion and its causes have not yet been studied closely. At no point in that century was there any single idea of race acceptable to all scholars, and yet by the time the century ended very many people identified themselves and others in racial terms.

The doctrine of racial types was pre-Darwinian. It could make no allowance for the way in which forms of life transported to another part of the world could, by changing, adapt to that new environment. The theory of natural selection was able to account for the evidence about differences between humans as part of a comprehensive explanation of diversity and change throughout the natural world. Darwin's book *On the Origin of Species by Means of Natural Selection, or the Preservation of Favoured Races in the Struggle for Life* was published in 1859. In the fourth edition, Darwin referred to 'geographical races or subspecies' as 'local forms completely fixed and isolated'. A subspecies was what had previously been called a variety. It was a division of a species consisting of individuals which differed in appearance from those in other divisions, but which could still mate with individuals in those other divisions, and produce fertile offspring should their isolation be broken down. If the word 'race' is used by biologists today, it is used in this sense.

Darwin described processes of selection, but he could not identify the unit upon which selection operated. That was the contribution made by Mendel when he experimented with the breeding of peas. Evolution comes about by the selection of genes. The 1930s saw the development of population genetics as a branch of study which took the gene rather than the species as the unit of selection and attributed to each gene a definite fitness value. By 1950 a textbook entitled *Genetics and the Races of Man* defined a race as 'a population which differs significantly from other human populations in regard to the frequency of one or more of the genes it possesses' (Boyd 1950: 207). Since it is now thought that there may be as many as a million different human genes, by that definition there could be a million races. In practice no one now draws this conclusion because it does not help biologists in the tasks with which they are engaged.

One task which does require biologists to classify humans is in connection with blood transfusions. Nineteenth-century racial classifications are useless for this purpose. Understanding of blood groups is essential. In 1900 the ABO system was discovered. Later research showed that in this system an individual's group was determined by three genes, A and B being dominant relative to O. Someone with two O genes has blood of group O. Someone with two A genes or one A and one O has blood of group A. Someone with two B genes or one B and one O, has blood of group B. Someone with one A and one B gene has blood of group AB. There are other systems too, and their utility can be illustrated by the Rhesus system, so named because it was first detected by immunizing rabbits with blood cells from Rhesus monkeys. About 16 per cent of Europeans are Rhesus-negative. When a Rhesus-negative woman has children by a Rhesus-positive man the children are likely to inherit both a D gene and a D antigen (an antigen can combine with antibodies in blood to make it change, for example, by clotting). Under certain conditions the mother's blood will produce an antibody called anti-D which can destroy the D-positive red cells in the foetus. The resulting anaemia used frequently to cause the baby's death, but now this can be prevented by transfusions of blood from a Rhesus-negative (i.e. D-negative) donor – that is, blood without the antibody. The heredity of blood groups, like that of eye colour, is determined by only a few genes, whereas the heredity of the shape, size, and colour of the body is determined in a complex way by a variety of genes and is also subject to the influence of diet and other environmental factors.

The frequency of blood group B is lower among Europeans than among Africans or Asians, but the differences are not very great. Among some American Indian populations there seem to be few if any people at all of this group, but for the most part the figures show continuous distributions. Moving across Europe and Asia, for example, the percentage of people of group B in England is 7.2; it rises to 11.2 in France, 12 in Germany, 14.2 in Bulgaria, 21.8 in Russia, and up to a peak in Central Asia before declining. Data of this kind demand that research workers calculate gene frequencies, not that they divide the populations into separate categories as if there were significant discontinuities in the figures. The old, Linnaean, kind of classification is of little use for solving the new problems uncovered by genetics. Nineteenth century anthropologists could not know this. They relied upon a method that had, apparently, been successful in arranging plants and animals into a systematic set of categories. It was an attempt to fit each individual specimen into the most appropriate space in a comprehensive scheme. It assumed that once a specimen's place had been determined, something new and important had been learned about that specimen. Unlike blood-group classification, there was no simple purpose behind the Linnaean classification or its nineteenth century extensions in respect of humans. Therefore there was little discussion of the elementary principle – which again can be illustrated by the various blood-group systems – that the same specimens might need to be classified differently for different purposes.

ETHNICITY

Classification in everyday life does not follow the same principles as classification in the laboratory. People give to themselves names which show who they claim to be rather than who they actually are. They give to others names which show how they perceive these others, and which may differ from the names the others have for themselves. The names show they identify themselves by religion or nationality more often than by race. Ethnic names are a variant of national names. A national group is created when people successfully maintain that because of their common character their members constitute a nation and should be a separate state. An ethnic group is similar except that when its members are a minority they do not demand separate political institutions. Only within the last half-century have ethnic names come into use and there is still some uncertainty about how they are best differentiated from other sorts of names. Much of the uncertainty arises because in everyday life ethnic names are influenced by the politics of group relations, while in the context of social science research the purposes of ethnic classification are still those of a general sorting out of specimens like the classifications of eighteenth-century natural history.

In the use of ethnicity for naming groups, two tendencies have recently been apparent. The first is to regard ethnicity as an attribute of minorities. In Britain, the English have regarded the Scots, Welsh, Gujeratis, Afro-Caribbeans, Poles, etc., as groups defined by ethnic attributes. The English have not regarded themselves as an ethnic group because, being the largest group and the dominant element in the population, there has been no pressure upon them to ask what

23

makes them distinctive. Only if they go to some country where they are a minority do they start to ask that question. Their outlook is an example of 'minus one ethnicity,' so called because when members of the dominant group add up the number of ethnic groups in their country they count all the groups except their own. In the United States it has long been customary to speak of Irish-Americans, Italian-Americans, Polish-Americans, and so on. Only recently has the expression 'Anglo-American' made an appearance. Because it takes itself for granted, the dominant group usually identifies itself by the name of the nation. In New Zealand the main population division is that between the people of Maori and European descent. The latter are known as Pakehas, using the Maori name for stranger. So most people there can claim the national name, New Zealander, and an ethnic name, Maori or Pakeha. The position can be contrasted with that in Scandinavia where there are national names, Norwegian, Swedish, and Finnish. There is also an ethnic minority in the North who used to be called Lapps but who call themselves Sami. They have national names depending upon the state in which they live, and an ethnic name, Sami. The majority population in each of the three countries identifies itself by a national name only and is under no pressure to wonder whether it has an ethnicity, or to coin an ethnic name.

The second tendency has been the assumption that racial groups are distinguished by appearance and ethnic groups by cultural characteristics, such as language, history, customs, shared attitudes, etc. Thus ethnic groups may be subdivisions of racial groups. Irish-, Italian-, and Polish-Americans may be seen as ethnic subdivisions of the racial category white American. In Britain, Irish, Scots, and Welsh may be seen as ethnic subdivisions of a racial category which might be called either European or white. Then there are subdivisions defined in racial terms because their appearance differs from that of the majority, such as Afro-Americans and Native Americans, or, in Britain, Afro-Caribbeans and South Asians. The British now lump together all the Afro-Caribbeans as blacks. They often recognize a racial subdivision comprising all the South Asians, though they may call its members either Indians or Pakistanis according to whether there are more people from one or the other country in the locality. Members of these minorities may define themselves differently from the way in which they are defined by others. This will require discussion later, but the first question to consider is whether popular ideas about what differentiates racial from ethnic groups constitute an adequate basis for differentiating

24

them in social science? In science, old-style racial classifications have been superseded by classifications based in genetics. To give social groups racial names is to keep alive old ideas that should be forgotten. The contrary argument is that, whatever one calls them, differences of physical appearance have consequences for social relations that are more inflexible and wide-reaching than differences of culture. Most people have no option about whether others will classify them as black, brown, white, or yellow. It is an involuntary assignment to a social category, and it puts a lot of pressure upon individuals to identify themselves with that category. Cultural characteristics are different in that the child of immigrant parents is not obliged to identify with his or her parents' homeland or to speak its language. To get him or her to do this, there has to be a social organization which offers emotional and/or material rewards to those who maintain the cultural characteristics of the migrant homeland instead of conforming to the expectations of people in the new country.

The conventional distinction between racial groups as physically defined and ethnic groups as culturally defined, is not altogether satisfactory for sociological purposes. It takes no account of the way that a minority defined by others as racial may at the same time have ethnic characteristics. The same set of people can constitute both a racial and an ethnic minority, just as they can also be a linguistic minority and a religious minority. In some circumstances it is necessary to start from a group's self-definition, in others with the way a group is defined by other people. Members of a group may disagree with one another about the best self-definition and may also disagree about the names by which others are to be designated. Here again, social organization operates as a variable between the facts about a person's ancestry and an individual's own preferences as to names. Societies are organized in ways that make physical features relevant to behaviour in certain situations and which determine how people of intermediate appearance are classified. Popular ideas about physical classification are themselves influenced by social and cultural pressures.

RACISM

At the beginning of the chapter it was asserted, with reference to race, that it is wrong to assume that because there is a word there must be something which corresponds to it. That same argument also applies to the word 'racism'. This entered the European languages in the early 1930s and was first used to identify the doctrine that race determines culture. The underlying concept of race was that of race as type. Some types were supposed to be permanently superior in their ability to generate civilization. In the late 1960s in the United States it was given an extended meaning as designating the use of racial beliefs and attitudes to subordinate and control a category of people defined in racial terms. The word was then increasingly used to express a moral judgement. Anything which could be called racist was by definition bad. A concept had become an epithet. A third use of the word 'racism' was as a label for a historical complex, generated within capitalism, facilitating the exploitation of categories of people defined in racial terms. At first this complex was called racial prejudice, but by 1970 it was generally referred to as racism. One objection to this definition is that there are similar complexes in Japan and other regions where they cannot have been caused or developed by capitalism. Racism is also used in a fourth, much more general sense, to refer to almost anything connected with racial discrimination, prejudice, inequality, or with apartheid. Thus when the press reported the death of President Samora Machel of Mozambique in 1986 he was described as a fighter against racism when he could have been called a fighter against white supremacy or against apartheid. A Brent headmistress alleged to have said that she did not want a black teacher posted to her school was constantly said to have 'made a racist remark', when what she allegedly said would have been more accurately described as expressing a wish to discriminate. This variability makes it more difficult to use the word 'racism' with precision in social science and leads some writers to distinguish biological, cultural, economic, political, and other kinds of racism. It neglects the distinction between racism as something associated with physical differences and ethnocentrism as a form of bias that reflects the preconceptions of a particular ethnic community. All groups show some ethnocentrism, but it is never claimed that all groups show some degree of racism.

The political power of racism as an epithet, and the difficulty of agreeing a definition, was illustrated at the United Nations (UN) in 1975 when the representative of Kuwait introduced resolution 3379 declaring 'Zionism is a form of racism and racial discrimination'. It was a major step in a campaign by Arab states against Israel and the movement, Zionism, which had created that state. The originators of the motion did not draw any distinction between racism and racial discrimination; they saw the two as aspects of the same thing in line with the second, late 1960s, definition just quoted. They argued that under Israel's law only Jews could be proper citizens in Israel and that since Jews were a race, the Israeli state was racist. Their arguments were criticized by Daniel Patrick Moynihan, the United States Ambassador to the UN, who was himself a social scientist. He operated with the first definition, of racism as a doctrine, and quoted *Webster's Third New International Dictionary* which defined it as 'the assumption that ... traits and capacities are determined by biological race and that races differ decisively from one another'. According to the *Dictionary*, racism also involved 'a belief in the inherent superiority of a particular race and its right to domination over others'. Moynihan maintained that the assumption and the belief to which the *Dictionary* referred were both alien to Zionism. He described this as a movement, established in 1897, which was to persons of the Jewish religion a Jewish form of what others called national liberation movements.

Moynihan stated that 'racial discrimination is a practice, racism is a doctrine'. The UN had defined racial discrimination, but not racism. The allegation that Zionism was a form of racism was, he said 'incomparably the more serious charge'. One of the few occasions on which racism had been discussed at the UN was in 1968 in connection with the International Convention on the Elimination of All Forms of Racial Discrimination. Speaking very sarcastically of the intellectual precision with which the matter was being treated, Moynihan described the discussion on that occasion about the order in which 'racism' and 'Nazism' should be mentioned in a preambular paragraph:

> The distinguished representative of Tunisia argued that 'racism' should go first because, he said, Nazism was a form of racism. Not so, said the no less distinguished representative of the Union of Soviet Socialist Republics, for, he explained, Nazism contained all the main elements of racism within its ambit, and should be mentioned first. That is to say that racism was merely a form of Nazism .... If, as the distinguished representative declared, racism is a form of Nazism, and if, as this resolution declares, Zionism is a form of racism, then we have step by step taken ourselves to the point of proclaiming – the United Nations is solemnly proclaiming – that Zionism is a form of Nazism.

This playing with words was intellectually dishonest. It was also dangerous for minorities which depended on laws to protect their rights. Moynihan's protest was eloquent:

> Today we have drained the word racism of its meaning. Tomorrow, terms like 'national self-determination' and 'national honour' will be

27

perverted in the same way to serve the purposes of conquest and exploitation. And when these claims begin to be made, as they have already begun to be made, it is the small nations of this world whose integrity will suffer. And how will the small nations of the world defend themselves, and on what grounds will others be moved to defend and protect them, when the language of human rights, the only language by which the small can be defended, is no longer believed and no longer has a power of its own?

The resolution at the UN has been used for political ends in other places. In Britain the National Union of Students in 1974 decided that students' unions should not allow racists and Fascists to address meetings on their premises. Following the UN, student unions refused to recognize the formation of Jewish societies 'to promote greater understanding of the Jewish religion, culture and people, the state of Israel and Zionism'. They declared that such a programme was by definition racist. The National Union of Students then threatened to suspend these unions if they persisted in this interpretation of the policy.

It is possible to discuss the sociology of racial relations without using the word 'racism'. Other words, like racial discrimination, prejudice, incitement, doctrine, ethnocentrism, and so on, are sufficient for almost any purpose. If people wish to use the word they should recognize that there is an important difference between describing actions or statements as racist, and describing people as racist. To tell someone that his or her actions are racist is to suggest that he or she is capable of behaving in some other manner. It is to suggest that the propriety of the action can be discussed and that the parties might come to an agreement about the best way to behave in future. To tell someone that he or she is racist is to imply that there is something wrong with the actor rather than the action. It drives the person into a corner and reduces the likelihood that he or she will behave differently in future. This is a political tactic and is to be distinguished from the attempts of social scientists to develop a concept of racism that could illuminate the causes of racial tension.

CHAPTER 3

Groups and individuals

One person belongs to many groups. People identify themselves with others on the basis of class, gender, language, religion, and so on. Others assign them to social categories on a corresponding basis. The importance of any one kind of membership varies according to the individual and his or her circumstances, while the various bases for identification have different implications. The nature of class consciousness, and the bonds based upon it, are matters of dispute which need not be discussed here. Few, though, would dispute that differences of language and religion inevitably give rise to groups and to the recognition of divisions between them. Differences of gender are scarcely likely to disappear either, but it is conceivable that in some society, some day, differences of complexion may have no more social significance than differences of eye colour and height have in contemporary Britain. If people were more enlightened they would classify others in ways that reflected whether they were good or bad citizens rather than by reference to attributes that are fixed and bear no relation to individual qualities. Racial consciousness is a feature of group contact that could be reduced to the level of insignificance. Justice requires that social status reflect individual merit rather than the accidents of birth. To discover how racial consciousness may be reduced it is necessary first to find out what has made it so prominent a feature of international relations and of relations within those societies that are called multiracial.

Racial consciousness reflects the contact between people who can be distinguished by their physical appearance, but there are important parallels with contacts between peoples distinguished by cultural features like language and religion. British history can be seen as the invasion of the country by Angles, Saxons, Normans,

Huguenots, etc., and the interaction between the English, Welsh, and Scots leading to a situation in which most of the differences have disappeared. This is not always the case. The people known as Greeks settled in many parts of what is now Turkey and in other regions to the east. Constantinople was a Greek city until it fell to the Ottoman Turks in 1453. Under Ottoman rule Greeks and other minorities, often distinguished by religion, remained distinct over the centuries. The negotiations for a political settlement after the First World War led to fighting between Greece and Turkey and this caused the flight of a large Greek refugee population from Turkey, Bulgaria, and Russia. In 1923 there was an official population exchange between Greece and Turkey in which Greece received some 1,300,000 refugees in return for 380,000 people considered Turkish. More than six centuries of contact had not led to the disappearance of the differences between these groups. Consciousness of group membership had remained significant. This history, like that of Cyprus, shows the importance of the political framework (and the link between religion and politics) in influencing what happens as a result of group contact. In some structures contact leads to the reduction of differences, whether cultural or (as in the case of Brazil, for example), physical; in others those differences are maintained. The effect of contact also varies between sectors of society. In sectors which do not affect the balance of power (like recreation or cuisine) or which facilitate the objectives of the superordinate group (like language and education) differences are more easily reduced. When it is a question of group control over economic resources or gainful occupations differences may be maintained.

EUROPEAN EXPANSION

Some of the major forms of contemporary racial consciousness are the outcome of the process by which Europeans established themselves in the New World in the sixteenth century; then on the coastline of West and South Africa, and in the Indian subcontinent. The Europeans differed from the native groups in their physical appearance and in respect of their work motivations and skills, like literacy and technical knowledge, particularly in the ability to use firearms. The Europeans were agents of relatively large and well-ordered states with the power of those states behind them. The native peoples were often organized in states, sometimes with a single monarch ruling a substantial territory, but these states were relatively small and could not mobilize so much power. The effect of this European presence, nevertheless, was to encourage native political organization on a larger scale with forms resembling those of the European state.

To start with, the differences seemed sharp. One group consisted of people who have been called white; the other of people who were black or coloured; there was a discontinuity in some ways comparable to the division of humans into males and females. The effect of contact was to reduce the discontinuities of appearance and of cultural attitudes, and to turn them into continuities. The distinction between discontinuous and continuous distributions (already mentioned in Ch. 2) is important here again. This is illustrated in Fig. 3.1. Figure 3.1(a) represents the situation in many English school and university classrooms: most people in the class are of fair complexion. Figure 3.1(b) typifies that to be found in some areas of minority settlement: a bimodal distribution with two large groups of fair and dark complexion and a number of intermediate appearance.

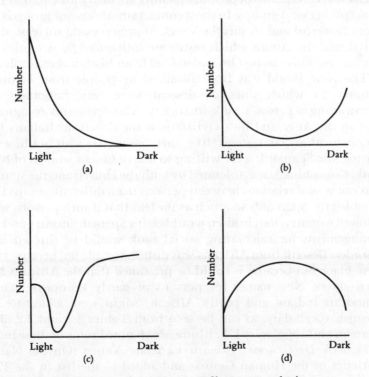

Figure 3.1 Distribution of persons according to complexion

Figure 3.1(c) represents the kind of development that might be expected overseas as a result of European invasion and settlement, while Fig. 3.1(d) represents a unimodal distribution of a kind that might be found in some parts of Latin America. The purpose of these comparisons is to show that differences in complexion constitute a continuous distribution whereas differences, say, of gender do not. It would make no sense to try to prepare a graph to show degrees of gender, with the most masculine individuals at one end, the most feminine at the other, and a range of intermediates. Gender is discontinuous and if the numbers of males and females in a class are to be represented visually this has to be by a block diagram, or histogram, with one column of a height that shows the proportion of males and another column the proportion of females.

The graphs in Fig. 3.1 show the distribution of persons as if their complexions had been measured scientifically. In everyday life matters are different. A continuous line is divided up into sections, and names like white, coffee-coloured, and black are given to segments. Perceptions of people's identity are then influenced by folk concepts of racial groups. In most contact situations one group is the more powerful and its members seek to preserve and increase their privileges; the groups which result are influenced by struggles for advantage. This can best be understood from historical examples.

The New World was first colonized by people from Spain, a country in which lines of descent were very important for determining a person's rank in society. The Spaniards recognized that in the Aztec and Inca civilizations the American Indians had hierarchical social systems like their own. To start with, even aristocratic Spaniards were willing to marry Indian women of high rank. Concubinage was tolerated by both the church and the state. It was not sexual relations between persons from different groups that troubled the Spaniards so much as the fear that if such persons were allowed to marry, the children would claim Spanish ancestry and the arrangements for calculating social rank would be thrown into disorder. Descent from Africans was dishonourable not because they were black but because it could be presumed that the Africans had been slaves. New names for persons of partly European, partly American Indian, and partly African origin were added to the Spanish vocabulary, as can be seen from Tables 3.1 and 3.2. The German anthropologist J. F. Blumenbach noted some of these in his 1775 book *De Generis Humani Varietate Nativa* (On the Native Varieties of the Human Genus) and added to the list in the 1795 edition from which Table 3.3 has been prepared. Some Spanish

Table 3.1   Names for persons of mixed origin in eighteenth century New Spain (i.e. the northern Spanish territories in the New World)

1. Spaniard and Indian woman beget mestizo
2. Mestizo and Spanish woman beget castizo
3. Castizo woman and Spaniard beget Spaniard
4. Spanish woman and Negro beget mulatto
5. Spaniard and mulatto woman beget morisco
6. Morisco woman and Spaniard beget albino
7. Spaniard and albino woman beget toma atrás
8. Indian and toma atrás woman beget lobo
9. Lobo and Indian woman beget zambaigo
10. Zambaigo and Indian woman beget cambujo
11. Cambujo and mulatto woman beget albarazado
12. Albarazado and mulatto woman beget barcino
13. Barcino and mulatto woman beget coyote
14. Coyote woman and Indian beget chamiso
15. Chamiso woman and mestizo beget coyote mestizo
16. Coyote mestizo and mulatto woman beget ahí te estás

(*Source:* Mörner 1967: 58)

Table 3.2   Names for persons of mixed origin in eighteenth century Peru

1. Spaniard and Indian woman beget mestizo
2. Spaniard and mestizo woman beget cuarterón de mestizo
3. Spaniard and cuarterona de mestizo beget quinterón
4. Spaniard and quinterona de mestizo beget Spaniard or requinterón de mestizo
5. Spaniard and Negress beget mulatto
6. Spaniard and mulatto woman beget quarterón de mulatto
7. Spaniard and cuarterona de mulatto beget quinterón
8. Spaniard and quinterona de mulatto beget requinterón
9. Spaniard and requinterona de mulatto beget white people
10. Mestizo and Indian woman beget cholo
11. Mulatto and Indian woman beget chino
12. Spaniard and chino beget cuarterón de chino
13. Negro and Indian women beget sambo de Indio
14. Negro and mulatto woman beget zambo

(*Source:* Mörner 1967: 58–9)

writers elaborated long lists of names for many sorts of possible mixture, but it is doubtful whether they were much used in everyday life. Nevertheless, their multiplicity must have made it easier for people to accept that group distinctions were matters of degree. In Spanish-speaking parts of America no sharp line is drawn between black and white. For a long time the trend has been, and still is,

Table 3.3 The principal names for human hybrids listed by Blumenbach in 1795

First generation	
European + Ethiopian	Mulatto
European + American	Mestizo
Ethiopian + American	Zambo
Second generation	
European + mulatto	Terceron or quarteron
European + mestizo	Castiso
Mulatto + mulatto	Casqua
Ethiopian + mulatto	Griff
American + zambo	Zambaigi
Third generation	
European + terceron	Quarteron
European + castiso	Postiso
Mulatto + terceron	Saltatra
Mulatto + zambaigi	Cambujo
Quarteron + mestizo	Coyota
Griff + zambo	Givero
Fourth generation	

'... there are those who extend even into the fourth generation this kind of pedigree, and say that those born from Europeans from Quarterons of the third generation are called Quinterons, in Spanish Puchuelas, but this name is also applied to those who are born of Europeans and American Octavons.'

(*Source:* Blumenbach 1865: 216–18)

towards the kind of distribution shown in Fig. 3.1(d), not only in appearance but also in social position.

The case of Brazil is the more interesting because a larger proportion of slaves were brought there from Africa than were brought to the Spanish colonies apart from Cuba. Brazil was a colony of Portugal from 1534 to 1822 when it became independent under its own emperor, the Prince Regent of Portugal. He and his successor ruled until 1889 when the country became a republic. Brazil experienced rapid economic growth over short periods with a sequence of successful export products. During these times there was a strong demand for African slaves. But the booms were punctuated by periods of depression in which the value of slaves declined and many of the older and less valuable were given their freedom. There was also a population of mulattos descended from unions between Portuguese men and African women. They secured a special niche in the socio-economic structure as the agents of whites in supervising slaves (in agriculture and mining), pursuing those that ran off, making war upon local Indian groups and escaped slave settlements, serving as urban artisans, boatmen, and cattle herdsmen. This created the 'mulatto escape hatch' whereby these men and women escaped from the bottom tier of society and secured intermediate positions. In this way there developed a continuous distribution of status in which complexion was one criterion among others. Partly in consequence, the emancipation of slaves was a gradual process. In 1871 a statute required the registration of all 1,700,000 slaves and the emancipation of those in certain categories. In 1885 those aged over 60 years were brought within these provisions; by this time it was impossible to maintain a slave code that lacked any moral sanction, so that in 1888 the remainder were freed without any compensation being paid to their former owners.

In the early period of the settlement of Brazil, as of the United States, slavery assisted economic development because it provided a labour force at a time when labour was scarce. Since land was readily available, free labourers were inclined to go off and farm for themselves, so a system of unfree labour was advantageous in binding workers to the large-scale production units necessary to produce export crops. In the long run, though, slave labour was less productive than free labour because a man will work hardest when he is working for himself. It was uneconomic to use capital to purchase labour once wage-labour became available: wage-labourers did not have to be fed, housed, and looked after in times of sickness; if they died the employer had not lost his capital. Societies built upon slave labour had to undergo fundamental change once the economic balance tipped and slavery became uneconomic. In Brazil the transition was gradual; in the United States it came about only after a bitter four-year civil war.

CONTINUOUS AND DISCONTINUOUS RANKING

A clear colour line between black and white was drawn in the United States because the whites had the power to draw it. Relations between blacks and whites were polarized and, especially in the Deep South, a discontinuous distribution of racial status was established. Whites might have done the same in Brazil (and in Latin America generally) if they had similar opportunities, but it suited them to make more allowance for variations in individual talents. What happens today in parts of Brazil may be explained, very crudely, by reference to the idea of a continuous scale in which complexion is only one element in this computation of status. It is as if, when one man meets another, he obtains an impression of the other's wealth and education; he judges him from his mode of dress, speech, and complexion, giving him imaginary points on a series of scales. If the other man is a dark-complexioned lawyer, he might score 6 out of 10 on wealth, 9 on education, 8 on costume, and 1 on complexion, an average of 6. In Brazil he would rank above a fair-complexioned bank cashier who scored 3, 5, 4, and 8 on these scales (if wealth were more important than the other criteria, that scale could be weighted more heavily by calculating its points out of a larger maximum; it is the principle which matters not the technique). In the United States the lawyer would have been assigned to the black category. His points would have given him a high rank in that category, but in most inter-racial situations they would not have enabled him to outrank the white bank cashier. There was discontinuity in the calculation of rank reflecting the existence of two hierarchies. The separation between the two was maintained by the whites chiefly in the circumstances which they defined as relating to social equality, but it was often ignored in business relations. In recent times the range of situations defined in business terms has increased so that the pattern of continuous rank has been gaining over the discontinuous one. The latter, which had its classic expression in the Deep South, has often been called 'colour-caste'. It employs a two-step procedure. In the first step an individual is assigned to either the black or the white category in accordance with his or her appearance. This is a discontinuous ranking because black–white is a yes–no kind of differentiation, unlike placing someone on a scale. The second step is one of continuous ranking within a category, by reference to wealth, education, speech, demeanour, and so on, in which high points on one scale compensate for low points on another. Among blacks in the United States a whole range of terms have been used to distinguish shades of complexion, but they were irrelevant to the way individuals aligned themselves in any situation in which the white category was opposed to the black.

It is important to appreciate that in different parts of the New World the same individuals' social positions would have been differently assessed. In Latin America a coffee-coloured man might be called a mulatto and be at a disadvantage compared with a white man, but rank ahead of a black man. In the Deep South the coffee-coloured man would have been assigned to the black category and in his dealings with whites would probably have enjoyed no advantage on account of his lighter complexion. A set of individuals corresponding to Fig. 3.1(d) would in Latin America, have been described by a large number of names referring to their individual shades of complexion. In the Deep South they would have been divided into two. The racial categories employed in everyday life both reflect and mould popular consciousness and they follow a different logic from that which directs classification in the biological sciences.

In societies in which appearance is one element in a continuous scale, a fair complexion has usually been preferred to a dark one. Thus when a survey in Puerto Rico in 1956–57 asked respondents what was the best colour to have, nearly half replied white (or *blanco*, since the interviews were conducted in Spanish); 8 per cent said mulatto *(trigueno)* and just over 1 per cent black *(negro)*; nearly 40 per cent replied that there was no best colour because people were equal. When asked, 'Would you say that persons of your colour have more, the same, or less opportunity to make their way in life than persons of other skin colours?', over 76 per cent declared that everyone had the same opportunities irrespective of colour (though among the white respondents nearly 28 per cent thought their colour gave them an advantage). When asked, 'Would you say that persons of your colour are respected much more than, the same as, or less than persons of a different colour?', nearly 87 per cent said that people received the same respect regardless of their colour. These replies are analysed according to respondents' views as to the colour categories in which they themselves belonged, in Table 3.4(A). The answers do not explain why so many should consider everyone equal in terms of respect when so many thought white the best colour to have.

Another part of the puzzle is contributed by Table 3.4(B), which compares the number of persons in the sample who were judged by local interviewers (themselves of all colours) to be *blanco, trigueno,* or *negro,* with the number of respondents who assigned themselves to these categories. It will be seen that nearly 12 per cent of those considered white, and over 31 per cent of those considered black, preferred to call themselves mulatto. One possible explanation of these findings is that Puerto Ricans appreciated that a light complexion had conferred an advantage, and in some circumstances still did so, but that either consciously or unconsciously they recognized this as a source of injustice and reacted against any expectation that colour should influence social position. It is as if they thought it best to do away with the categories black and white and for everyone to be mulatto. This is a speculative interpretation. What is more convincing is that, as shown in Table 3.4(A), so few of the black respondents should have thought that they were accorded

Racial consciousness

Table 3.4   (A) Respect accorded to skin colour in Puerto Rico;
(B) Assignment to colour categories

Colour of respondent	More respect (%)	Some (%)	Less respect (%)	Ns* (000's)
(A)				
White	17.6	81.8	0.6	483
Mulatto	5.0	92.9	2.0	397
Black	9.4	84.9	5.7	53
Total	11.8	86.7	1.5	933

(B)	White	Mulatto	Black
Interviewer's assignment	608	307	80
Self-assignment	537	397	55

Note: The totals of these two tables vary because some respondents did not provide usable replies to the question about respect.
*Total size of division.
(Source: Tumin 1961: 227–46)

less respect because of their colour. Physical differences are not always a basis for drawing distinctions.

The contrast between Puerto Rico and the Deep South is a contrast in the importance of individual relative to group attributes. The possibility of grouping by colour is recognized in Puerto Rico, but it is not a basis for social roles. In the Deep South individual attributes were completely subordinated to group membership in situations of racial conflict, but at other times people responded to the other person's individual qualities as well as to racial categorization. Groups are composed of individuals whose behaviour can bring about change in the character of the groups themselves. Yet the individuals have been profoundly influenced by the groups within which they have been brought up and with which they identify. Group and individual influences are at work in all situations but the balance between them varies. In parts of Mexico, for example, an individual man can choose to be either an Indian or a mestizo. He can live with Indians, speak an Indian language, dress in Indian clothes, and use an Indian name. Or he can live like a mestizo. It is choice rather than colour that decides the issue, though choice may be subjected to the constraints of kinship and past friendship.

In Central America there has been a process of *mestizaje* (or mestizization) which seems to be exemplified in the Puerto Rican finding than 12 per cent of whites and over 31 per cent of blacks regarded themselves as mulattos. The trend probably reflects individual advantage (mestizos being subject to less discrimination), the feeling that this is the direction in which the society is moving, and a tendency to elevate the highest common factors of national identification. It can be helpful to envisage group changes as the aggregation of sets of individual changes. As an index of the *mestizaje* of an Indian group it would be possible to ascertain the proportion of individuals able to speak Spanish, or speaking Spanish at home, and plot these numbers on a chart to show changes over time. This could be represented by a diagram like that in Fig. 3.2 which plots over time the linguistic change in the use of Welsh. A diagram to show the increasing use of Spanish by Indians in Mexico would contain a rising curve to show the proportion of persons able to speak Spanish and a falling curve for those able to speak only an Indian language. The first curve could be described as a measure of the assimilation of Indians to Spanish culture in respect of language, but it has to be remembered that, as the Puerto Rican study showed, *mestizaje* also affects whites. The version of Spanish spoken in Latin America now differs from Castilian Spanish. People of Spanish origin in Latin America have been influenced by Indian culture in their ways of life and national identification. When groups of different culture come together in new political units there is a two-way process by which differences are reduced.

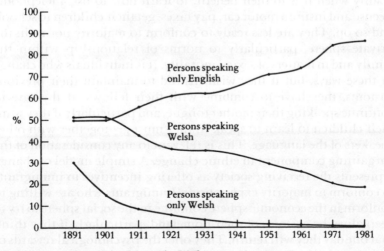

Figure 3.2 Linguistic change in Wales

ASSIMILATION

It is appropriate to call this process assimilation, in the dictionary sense of 'becoming similar', although this sometimes occasions misunderstanding since many people now take assimilation to be a process by which one group absorbs another without itself being changed. The sociological concept of assimilation passed into ordinary language in the United States at a time when white Americans were anxious that immigrants from eastern and southern Europe might not make good citizens. It was equated with Americanization and with changes by minorities to conform with majority expectations. The same distortion has been apparent in British usage since the 1950s, in that assimilation has often been equated with Anglicization. Sociological usage has, in turn, been influenced by the word's popular meaning. This has supported an idea of 'straight line' assimilation in which all aspects of minority life are under pressure to conform to majority conventions. Critics have very rightly pointed out that minorities may adopt the language of the majority and all the practices necessary to earn a living in the new society while maintaining their own religion and many of the practices important in their private lives. Trends such as those of language change are an aggregation of individual choices.

Immigrants in a new country often find that to get work they need to speak the language of that country. In this, and in many other respects, they accept the need to conform to majority ways. They do so readily when it is to their benefit: to learn how to use a telephone, license and insure a motor car, pay taxes, get their children to school, and so on. They are less ready to conform to majority norms in the private sphere, particularly to norms of relationship within the family and in matters of sexual morality. It is individuals who change in these ways, but if they wish instead to maintain their previous customs, they have to combine with their fellows. If they are to continue speaking their mother tongue, and particularly if they want their children to learn to speak it, they must get together with other speakers of the language. This is relevant to any consideration of the bargaining component in ethnic change. A simple model of change represents the receiving society as offering incentives to immigrants to conform to majority expectations. Immigrants who are willing to conform in the economic sphere combine in the social sphere to try to keep alive the customs of their homeland, particularly if they think that one day they will return. They offer the psychological rewards of esteem and affection to those of their number who observe the old customs and help maintain an immigrant community. The majority society often finds that it has to reward minority members in order to obtain their loyalty, or to threaten sanctions for disloyalty. The participants do not see this as a bargaining process, but from the outside it is apparent that individuals are exercising choices between alternatives. To this has then to be added the collective dimension. Some objectives can be attained only by collective action. If, for example, they want to agitate against discrimination, minority people must organize, offering to support political parties that will favour their cause and threatening to campaign against those that will not. Here the bargaining is explicit. If young blacks in Brixton or Haringey organize to attack the police their conduct may be interpreted as implicit bargaining. It is as if they said, 'We think we are being harassed and propose to retaliate. We will do this again if the police do not leave us in peace.' It is pressure of this kind, and from many directions, which causes outwardly harmonious relations to move towards conflict, and then find a new equilibrium.

Minority organization will be strong when the incentives for minority members to conform to majority expectations are weak. In some situations the members of a superordinate group discourage any tendencies for members of the subordinate group to adopt their ways because they assume that it is to their advantage to prevent assimilation. In the Deep South the pattern of incentives reinforced the colour line. Changes in the relations between the black and white groups could be brought about only by collective action whereby the power of the federal government was used to counterbalance the policies of state and local governments. There are similarities between the Deep South and other two-category societies in which everyone is assigned to either the superordinate category (call it P) or the subordinate category (B). Since they have shared interests to pursue, the individuals organize as two competing groups. The interaction constitutes a dynamic system which is the product of a set of forces. When group P can muster sufficient strength to prevent group B from changing the relations between the two groups, and group B can prevent group P from doing the same, then intergroup relations are in equilibrium. The strength that each group can muster is the product of relations within the group.

Relations rarely stay in equilibrium for long because opinion within groups shifts. Changes in the society's environment (like the discovery or exhaustion of natural resources or alterations in world trade) may work to the relative advantage or disadvantage of either group. Figure 3.3 depicts possible consequences of change. The

41

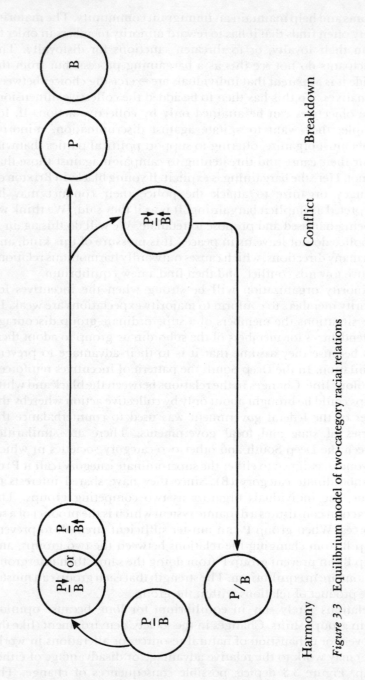

Figure 3.3 Equilibrium model of two-category racial relations

sequence starts on the left with a situation of harmony, in the sense that there are no signs of struggle between the two groups. It then changes, either because P seeks to extend its relative advantage over B by acquiring a greater share of the resources (indicated by the downward arrow indicating pressure from P), or because B seeks to reduce its relative disadvantage by obtaining a more even share of resources (indicated by the upward arrow indicating pressure from B). This upsets the equilibrium between P and B. Signs of struggle increase. One possible outcome is a breakdown of the system, by the expulsion of the losing party, by partition, or by the spread of disorganization. Partition is represented by the two separate circles for P and B. Another possible outcome is a conflict in which P and B mobilize their respective resources and then resolve the conflict by returning to a new equilibrium in which either B accedes to a deterioration in its position because of P's demands, or P accepts an improvement in B's relative position. The sources of change lie in the individuals' satisfaction or dissatisfaction with their relative positions, but the process of mobilization requires effective leadership. If one group acts in a way that outrages the expectations of people in the other group it may be easier to get members of that group to unite in collective action.

One of the skills of a political leader is the ability to seize upon an incident that can be turned to political advantage. Another important skill is the ability to bargain effectively. In any conflict between two racial groups, just as between an employer and a trade union, there may be a good moment for one side to offer a settlement. If that opportunity is not seized the price of harmony may increase. In interracial relations the bargaining is rarely conscious, but the superordinate group can often avoid conflict by making concessions before there is any trial of strength. By first sketching in Fig. 3.3 an abstract model of the elements involved in two-category racial relations it becomes possible to identify similarities between intergroup conflicts in quite different parts of the world, such as those between the Tutsi and Hutu in Rwanda and Burundi, discussed in Chapter 4, and those between blacks and whites in the United States and South Africa, discussed in Chapter 5.

CHAPTER 4
Peoples and states

Racial consciousness is much greater in societies in which appearance is used as a basis for discontinuous social classification. It is greatest when it evokes an identification of 'us' and 'them', and this is most potent when the groups differ in their power and their access to valued resources, like well-paying occupations. The study of racial consciousness, therefore, has to consider the political contexts within which peoples of different appearance have encountered one another. This, in turn, entails a historical perspective.

Some mid-nineteenth-century authors wrote of the 'swarming' of races as if each race at some point in its history sent out swarms of its members to colonize distant parts, just as bees and some other insects swarm at a point in their annual cycle. Many human societies have indeed passed through a phase in which they sent out their members and took over new territories. The Assyrians, Phoenicians, Persians, Romans, Turks, and Tatars did so in their time. From the fifteenth century many West European nations entered upon such a phase. Less is known about the ancient African empires built upon this principle, but there is no reason to think that they were very different and the Zulu provide a relatively modern example. In Asia the Mongols and the Han Chinese expanded to take over large territories. Consideration of such cases suggests that processes of expansion take two particular forms which can be called colonization and imperialism. Colonization is the planting of outposts in new territory. They may be trading-posts. They are enclaves within larger societies rather than centres from which people are ruled. This sense of the word survives in the way that, say, Italian restaurateurs, hairdressers, and other workers in a city like Bristol may be referred to as an Italian colony. Empire entails the sending out of individuals in order to rule other peoples. Imperialism cannot be defined with much precision. In the twentieth century the form which most often comes to mind is 'salt-water imperialism', the extension of power to rule peoples on the other side of an ocean. The extension of power by land, like Russian power in the Asian portion of the Soviet Union is not always counted as a form of imperialism. In modern times there has also been an extension of power by economic means rather than direct rule, and this has occasioned talk of 'dollar imperialism', 'neo-colonialism', and the like, but these notions are for use in the political arena. The distinction between colonization and imperialism has likewise been swallowed up in the tendency to speak of colonialism in a comprehensive sense.

IMPLICATIONS OF EMPIRE

The expansion of European power overseas took so many forms that generalization is hazardous. Nevertheless, for the purpose of an initial orientation it is possible to advance three propositions about the implications of empire for racial relations. The first is that *imperialism established a framework within which people who were previously strangers to one another could interact and do business.* It was a framework of peaceable rather than warlike relations. In Africa, fighting between ethnic (or 'tribal') groups was reduced both by the black empires and by the white ones. The latter regulated both inter-African (black–black) and inter-racial (black–white) relations. European states extended their rule in Africa for their own ends. They wanted to raise enough money to pay for the costs they incurred. They wanted to open up markets for their own merchants. They wanted to increase their influence in the world. They could do these things best if relations were peaceable. Within this framework new alliances were created between subgroups: white administrators with African chiefs, white traders with their black customers, white missionaries with black Christians, African intellectuals or trade-unionists of one ethnic group with their opposite number of another, and so on. Within this framework political structures were created that enabled Africans to form political parties and acquire political experience. The Europeans had created new political units by drawing lines on a map, but at the end of the imperial period these lines proved remarkably durable. In some places the people of one ethnic group are divided between two or three states (e.g. the Somalis in Somalia,

Ethiopia, and Kenya) but the new independent governments have been unwilling to revise these boundaries. That is testimony to the durability of the European influence which bequeathed to the late twentieth century a black Africa of some forty states instead of a much larger number of relatively small ethnic units. Imperial rule reduced a large number of small conflicts but left a small number of large ones.

Secondly, *imperialism incorporated ethnic groups differentially into new political structures.* One way in which this was sometimes done was to make overseas territories constitutionally part of the metropolitan country. In the early 1950s, for example, 29 deputies were elected from African (and other) constituencies who took seats in the National Assembly in Paris. Had the constituencies been drawn so that one deputy from Africa represented as many constituents as one deputy from France, there would have been not 29 but 390. That they had seats was an indication of their political incorporation. That they had fewer seats relative to their numbers, demonstrates that the incorporation was differential, or unequal.

A more common procedure was for the imperial power to create a subordinate form of government in the colonial dependency. The British pattern was the formation of a legislative council which could make laws for the colony. These laws had to be in accordance with British ideas of natural justice and could be disallowed if they were found offensive. The legislative council represented the people of the colony; it included representatives of European commercial interests and officials of the colonial administration. Some members were appointed by the Governor, but the trend over time was for members to be elected by popular vote so that the council had come to function as a parliament by the time of independence. Some colonies, like Kenya and Southern Rhodesia (now Zimbabwe) included areas suitable for European settlement. Other colonies, like most of West Africa, did not. In the former, white settlers often became politically powerful. The contrast between Northern Rhodesia (now Zambia) and Southern Rhodesia was particularly marked. In the former, political power remained with the British Crown and the country was administered by British officials who formed part of a colonial service with a career structure that could entail their being posted to Jamaica, Sierra Leone, or Hong Kong instead of staying where they were. Southern Rhodesia, by contrast, was initially under the control of the British South African Company, a private company operating under a royal charter. Though the British government established a legislative council in 1898, Southern Rhodesia did not formally become a Crown colony until 1923 when the whites voted against incorporation into the Union of South Africa. It became a partly independent state with its own career structure for administrators. In 1965 the governing party made a unilateral and illegal declaration of independence. Constitutionally, however, responsibility for the territory remained with the British government which was able to negotiate an end to the rebellion in 1979 and the transfer of power to a new government. The contrast between Northern and Southern Rhodesia could be represented as a contrast between imperialism and colonialism, since in the former there was an imperial administration whereas in the latter the interests of white colonists were politically dominant.

In both Northern and Southern Rhodesia Africans were differentially incorporated into the new political structures. In the former they were, after a while, represented on the legislative council, but whereas they constituted over 97 per cent of the population, it was not until independence that they had a correspondingly dominant position in the country's politics. In the period prior to independence African political movements were often called nationalist because they sought independence, just as, say, national movements in nineteenth-century Europe sought independence from Habsburg rule. It might have been more accurate to call the African movements anti-imperial or anti-colonial movements for there was relatively little sense of national belonging among the peoples of varied ethnic groups who had been brought into association by European imperialism. After independence the new states had to cultivate a sense of nationalism among their people in order to hold the societies together and to combat ethnic fragmentation. The first authentic African nationalism was that of the Afrikaners, the white settlers of Dutch origin who in the middle and late nineteenth century attempted to establish their own independent republics. If today the Zulu were to campaign for a separate state that, too, would be an illustration of nationalism. It would show a group of people with a distinct identity seeking to rule themselves, and no other peoples, in a territory which they claimed their own. Were that to happen, many would describe it not as nationalism but tribalism, because they would consider it politically retrograde. Third World nationalism in the latter part of the twentieth century is associated not with ethnic units but with states, and states are based upon the lines on the maps drawn in the latter part of the last century.

Thirdly, *when imperial rule ended, there was less friction if political power could be transferred either to non-ethnic political parties or to a dominant ethnic group*. Twentieth century transfers of power to non-ethnic political parties include such cases as Ghana in 1956, many West Indian countries around 1960, and Tanganyika (now Tanzania) in the following year. This category should also include Burma and India, despite the religious violence associated with Indian independence. Elsewhere power was transferred to the representatives of a political system which was formally non-ethnic, but in which one ethnic group, often because of its numerical strength, has a dominant influence upon the nature and administration of the system. Thus in Kenya, successive governments have been dominated by the Kikuyu. In Zimbabwe the Shona have established their primacy over the Ndebele. In Zaïre the Bakongo are pre-eminent, and in Pakistan the Pathans. In Guyana, the Creole or African half of the population have much greater political power than the Indian group of almost equal size. In Zanzibar the dominant group had been Arab from days before the British appeared. With economic growth more workers from the African mainland settled there and a political contest started which developed into polarization. The Arab-dominated Zanzibar National Party was opposed by a party of mainland Africans. Elections became flashpoints for racial violence. After independence in 1963, the African-led party experienced the frustration of winning a majority of votes but not a majority of seats. Shortly afterwards a mainland African led a revolutionary movement which set off a spate of racial brutalities. Several thousand Arabs were killed; by murder, repatriation, and emigration their numbers were reduced by over 20 per cent. So it was that there, as in some other countries, the numerically preponderant ethnic group asserted its claims.

RWANDA AND BURUNDI

The conflict in Zanzibar can be seen as an illustration of the changes represented by the equilibrium model of two-category relations shown in Fig. 3.3. To start with, relations were tranquil. Then the superordinate group was put under pressure by an increase in the size of the subordinate group and by intergroup competition in connection with elections. Conflict increased. The previously superordinate group had to lose some of its privileges before harmony was re-established. The whole system was changed by its incorporation into what then became Tanzania. The same model is illustrated more dramatically, and tragically, by events in the states of

Rwanda and Burundi to the west of Tanzania in the African interior (see map in Fig. 4.1). In 1899 they both became part of German East Africa, passing into Belgian hands in 1916 and being administered as a single unit by that country until their independence in 1962. Rwanda has a population of about 2.5 million, Burundi of 3.5 million. The population of both countries was composed of three strata, sometimes called castes, sometimes races, namely, the Twa, or forest-dwelling pygmies, who accounted for 1 per cent; the Hutu, or peasant cultivators, who made up 85 per cent; the Tutsi pastoralists, who had conquered the region in the sixteenth century and made themselves its rulers, constituted the remaining 14 per cent. The three groups have often been described by reference to typical representatives. Thus the Tutsi have been described as tall, graceful, and aristocratic; the Hutu as people whose 'ungainly figures, betoken hard toil, and who patiently bow themselves in abject bondage to the later arrived yet ruling race, the Tutsi'. Descriptions based upon typical representatives distract attention from the many people who do not correspond to any type. There were physical differences, the Tutsi being on average 1.75 metres tall (5 feet 10 inches) and the Hutu 1.66 metres (5 feet 6 inches), but the differences between the groups were mainly cultural and from their appearance many people could not be identified as either the one or the other.

In both Rwanda and Burundi there was an upper stratum and a lower. In the upper stratum were the King and the princes of the blood; within this élite the King was the first among equals, but since the dynastic families were rivals, the King could play one against another. The King found among the Hutu natural allies against the dynastic families, and he relied greatly on Hutu for the administration of his Crown lands. The Tutsi were divided by status and by region; the Hutu, being more numerous, were divided even more, but these divisions were balanced by patron–client relations linking all manner of people from the King to his lowest subject. One of the authorities on Burundi (Lemarchand and Martin 1974), concluded that although the traditional society contained a great many potential sources of conflict, in practice few if any conflicts followed ethnic lines. The ethnic massacres that occurred in 1972 were traceable to the social transformations of the twentieth century and to the distintegration of the traditional structures that once gave cohesion to society as a whole.

The overriding political problem was that of managing social and economic change so as to bring a society at a low level of development up to the standards being demanded at the UN. The Belgian

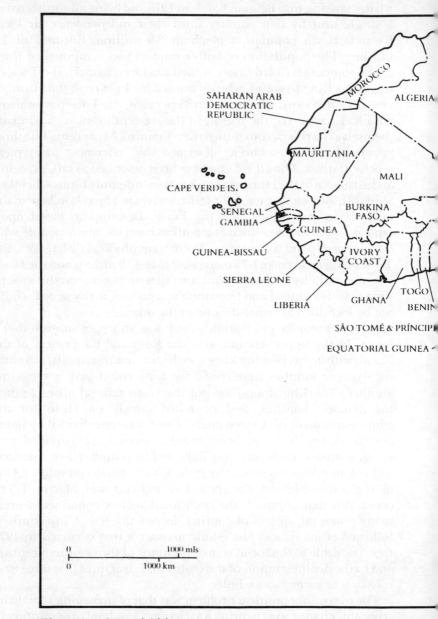

Figure 4.1   Map of Africa

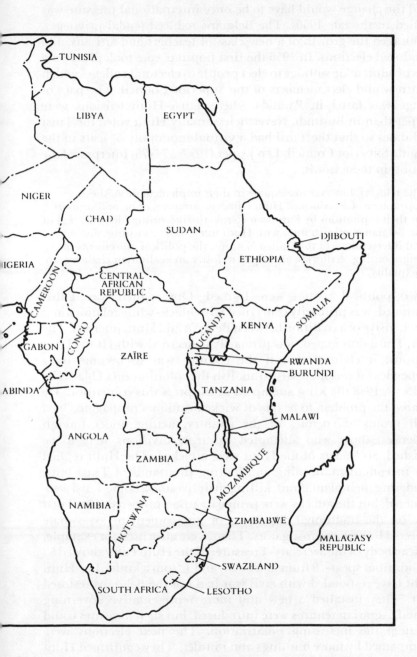

administration appreciated this, even if they could not foretell how rapid the change would have to be once international pressure was applied in the late 1950s. The Belgians reduced feudal privileges, encouraged the growth of a new class of teachers and artisans, and introduced elections. In 1956 the first popular vote took place on a basis of adult male suffrage to elect people to electoral colleges which in turn would elect members of the Superior Council. The pace of change was faster in Rwanda where Tutsi–Hutu tensions were sharper than in Burundi. Nevertheless, many Hutu voted for Tutsi candidates so that the Tutsi had a virtual monopoly of seats in the Rwanda Superior Council. Leo Kuper (1977: 174–75) interpreted the position in these words:

> The reforms, however inadequate in their implementation, the appearance of an educated Hutu élite, encouragement of, and support for their aspirations by European clergy, the increasing identification of the Belgian administration with Hutu interests, the visiting missions and interventions of the United Nations, the political movements in neighbouring territories, all helped to foster an egalitarian challenge to inequality.

Two political parties were formed. One, which was Tutsi-dominated, was primarily concerned with black–white relations and apprehensive of a coalition between Belgian and Hutu interests. The other, Hutu-dominated, was primarily concerned with Hutu–Tutsi relations; it claimed that if the country was to become truly independent it was necessary to abolish the colonization of blacks by blacks. In 1958 the King attempted to suppress this contention. He declared the problem to be one of wicked rumours propagated by a small group of enemies of the country, acting under foreign influences; those who attempted to create divisions were to be punished. So leaders of the Hutu were attacked. The Hutu replied with incendiarism, burning and looting thousands of Tutsi huts, plundering their plantations, killing their livestock. Some Tutsi were murdered, but the attacks were primarily upon property. The Tutsi drew on the traditional apparatus of government to assassinate suspected leaders and instigators. There were atrocities; for example, the dead body of the Secretary-Treasurer of the Hutu Party showed 53 wounds from spears, 9 from machetes, and 1 from a knife. The Hutu might have responded with civil war had not the Belgians restored order. They installed a new and more representative governing council. Agrarian reforms were introduced, but such measures could not stem the increasing polarization. The next elections were accompanied by more burnings and murder. They confirmed Hutu domination of the country by 1962, the date of independence. Tutsi leaders, removed from power inside the country, organized raids from across its frontiers, only to evoke reprisals even more severe. In one, Hutu massacred between 1,000 and 2,000 Tutsi men, women, and children, while a later and more general massacre took the total to over 10,000.

Rwanda now has a form of government acceptable to international opinion. It is a one-party state with a full panoply of laws formally proscribing discrimination based on race, colour, sex, religion, political opinion, national descent, or social origin. It has policies for the equitable allocation of jobs in the public and private sectors with quotas for each ethnic group, though it may not know whether the quotas are met. These objectives have been attained at an enormous cost in human lives and suffering. Rwanda's recent history illustrates one of the processes described in Fig. 3.3. To start with there was harmony between Hutu and Tutsi. Tension increased until there was open conflict and a possibility of breakdown. A Hutu revolution resulted in the expulsion of the previously ruling caste and the society moved round the flattened circle back to a new kind of harmony with the larger ethnic group in the politically dominant position.

Political change in neighbouring Burundi was much influenced by news of the violence in Rwanda. In Burundi the elections of 1961 were won by a party which stood for national unity, led by a royal prince who was popular among the Hutu. He was murdered. The Tutsi had difficulty accepting democratic reforms and relations were worsened by the actions of Tutsi refugees from Rwanda. In 1965 they murdered the Hutu Prime Minister. Despite their overwhelming success in the preceding elections, the Hutu were passed over in the selection of a new Prime Minister. An unsuccessful attempt at a coup was followed by Hutu terrorism and the murder of at least 500 Tutsi. As in Rwanda, this evoked reprisals on a larger scale. Somewhere between 2,500 and 5,000 Hutu were slain in 1965. There were repetitions in 1972 in which about 100,000 people or 3½ per cent of the population were massacred in the course of a few weeks. It has been described as selective genocide. It began with Hutu attacks upon Tutsi, but led to massive Tutsi counter-attacks and to the re-establishment of Tutsi rule. The Tutsi concentrated upon those Hutu who were, or might become, leaders. Soldiers and bands of Tutsi youth appeared in the classrooms of the university and at secondary schools with lists of Hutu names. Young people were loaded into trucks to be taken away. Few ever returned. Hutu pupils were assaulted by their Tutsi classmates and sometimes beaten to death.

Hutu priests were taken from the churches, and Hutu doctors and nurses from the hospitals. This was the selective element in the genocide. Though Hutu and Tutsi were often described, by themselves and by others, as races, they were not so distinctive that lists were not necessary to identify individuals. Prior to the killings there had been an open and flexible system of social stratification with considerable mobility. Afterwards there was a caste-like division; access to material wealth, status, and power being restricted to Tutsi.

The case of Burundi therefore exemplifies a different kind of circuit round the circle representing harmony and conflict in Fig. 3.3. Tension increased to open conflict, but the Hutu revolutionary movement was crushed. The previously ruling caste reasserted its domination and the society returned to a position of outward harmony on a more inegalitarian basis than before. This may be threatened by a new revolutionary challenge in the future.

The recent history of Rwanda and Burundi suggests that when a region is underdeveloped by international standards and has an inegalitarian social structure, change has to be gradual if it is to be peaceful. Such societies have a collectivistic character in that individuals are linked to others by a dense mesh of ties based upon kinship, clientage, and land-holding. To introduce elections in which voting is by individuals, is to open up a route for acquiring power and distributing resources that is in conflict with the traditional pattern. The example also suggests that no society can be isolated from the world outside. Colonial dependencies all became vulnerable to pressure organized through UN institutions; these bodies demanded a rate of change that made violence inevitable in regions like that of Rwanda and Burundi. Sociologists tend to emphasise the structural factors; with the advantage of hindsight, they regularly conclude that whatever happened, had to happen. It can be difficult for them to acknowledge that the course of change can also be influenced by the skill and personality of people in positions of leadership, by unpredictable assassinations, and the ability of leaders to make use of whatever opportunities arise. No one can be sure that so many people in Burundi had to die.

The Rwanda–Burundi example is significant in another respect. How were, and are, the Hutu and Tutsi best described? As castes? Races? Ethnic groups? There is no certain answer. It is the same problem as that mentioned early in Chapter 1 with the reference to Jews as a group with multiple characteristics. A distinctive appearance creates a category not a group, just as persons aged between 20 and 29 years, or persons earning between £20,000 and £29,000 per annum are categories and not groups. They can become groups if they organize to pursue shared interests or out of a feeling that they belong together. This feeling is more easily developed when a set of individuals have a lot of things in common – religion, language, history, a shared alignment *vis-à-vis* competitor groups, and so on. The Hutu and Tutsi were groups with a historical identity at the same time as individual members had important links with the members of the other group. It is a salutary lesson that these other links could so easily be broken by the pressures for polarization along ethnic lines. In other situations such as those of European rule in black Africa, there were important links relating individual Europeans to Africans (like administrator and chief, missionary and parishioner) and setting them against other people, European and African, but opposition easily polarized along the black–white division. Differences of skin colour have a special immediacy for social alignment because they can be seen at a distance and people can be assigned to categories without the need for enquiry into what they are like as individuals. They promote stereotyping and discrimination. People who have not themselves suffered from racial discrimination readily identify with those who have because they conclude 'it could have happened to me'. It is therefore exceedingly difficult to eliminate alignment in terms of colour. The best hope is not to deny its intrusiveness but to seek to highlight alternative bases for group alignment such as those of common religious beliefs and political allegiance.

GENOCIDE

Differences other than those of appearance have at times been magnified to the point at which members of another group have been regarded as subhuman, or as a kind of humanity so different that the ordinary rules are thought not to apply to them. They have made possible the crime of genocide. This is the name given to acts committed with intent to destroy, in whole or in part, a national, ethnic, racial, or religious group as such (the last two words are added to indicate that people are killed *because* they are members of such a group; it is a causal relationship, not simply an association). Genocide has at times been practised against quite inoffensive peoples when other groups wanted their land. The governments of

Brazil and Paraguay have been accused of genocide perpetrated against Indian groups in their territory. In reply, they have argued that whereas people may, without authorization, have attacked the Indians, the attacks were not directed against them because they were members of particular ethnic groups. The charge of genocide can more easily be brought against the Nazi government of Germany which was responsible for the slaughter of some 6 million Jews and about 250,000 Gypsies during 1941–45. The charge is also levelled against the government of Turkey for the deaths of about 800,000 Armenians in 1915. The killing of the Armenians took place as the Turks faced the threat of the dissolution of their empire; the Armenians had been struggling for greater independence, so their loyalty was in question. The destruction of the German Jews, however, was remarkable because they had moved further towards assimilating to the Gentile majority than Jews anywhere else; they posed no threat, but they proved convenient scapegoats.

Leo Kuper has summarized the major steps in the process as starting with the definition of who was a Jew. The identification of Jews by conspicuous symbols (such as being obliged to wear an armband bearing a Star of David in yellow), their expulsion from the Civil Service, the professions, responsible positions in business and industry, and the seizure of their property. They were vilified in political speeches, in publications, and through the mass media. To start with, the Nazi policy was to force Jews to emigrate, but about July 1941 the order was given for their extermination. Death camps were established on industrial principles. The victims were processed for slaughter as if on a conveyor belt. The camp staff, with bureaucratic efficiency, took into store the victims' possessions, their clothes, gold teeth, and women's hair; they arranged for their redistribution. Some killing centres were combined with slave camps where Jewish workers were treated as if they were expendable. Leading German firms established branches in the vicinity of the gas chambers and crematoria of Auschwitz.

Religious divisions can be the bases of cleavages which cut as deep as racial ones. Kuper also briefly described the violence which accompanied the partition of India and Pakistan when British rule ended in 1948. Tensions had been rising. The Muslim politicians have often been blamed for insisting that they had to have a separate state, but they could well have claimed that the violence only demonstrated the fears that lay behind their demand to have been justified. The state of Punjab was divided into two. In the village of Kahuta, where 2,000 Hindus and Sikhs and 1,500 Muslims had lived in peace, a Muslim horde set fire to the houses in its Sikh and Hindu quarters with buckets of petrol. Entire families were consumed by the flames. Those who escaped were caught, tied together, soaked with petrol, and burned alive. In Lahore, a previously tolerant city of some 500,000 Hindus, 100,000 Sikhs and 600,000 Muslims, a Sikh leader precipitated the violence with his cry of death to Pakistan. In the resulting riots 3,000 people were killed, mostly Sikhs. In the Sikh holy city of Amritsar, Hindus walked up to unsuspecting Muslims and threw vitriol or sulphuric acid into their faces. While the authorities performed the Independence Day rituals a horde of Sikhs was ravaging a Muslim neighbourhood only a short distance away. The men were slaughtered without mercy or exception. The women were repeatedly raped, then paraded through the streets to the Golden Temple where most of them had their throats cut. Muslims in the part of the Punjab that was to be Indian tried to move westwards across the boundary to Pakistan. Hindus and Sikhs in that area tried to move eastwards, but it was as dangerous to move as it was to stay. Refugee columns on the roads became targets for loot and massacre. On the railways trains were stopped by the assassins. There were periods of four and five days at a stretch when not a single refugee train reached Lahore or Amritsar without very many dead and wounded passengers. Since that time a religious movement among the Sikhs has generated a special brand of Sikh nationalism. There was a wave of assassinations of Hindus. The Indian army occupied the Golden Temple. Sikh zealots struck back. Mrs Indira Gandhi, the Indian Prime Minister, was assassinated. Killings continue. In 1987 when Sikh terrorists attacked Hindu buses, machine-gunning all the passengers, the government appealed to Hindus not to retaliate because the terrorists were deliberately inviting this, in the knowledge that further religious polarization would increase the chances of their obtaining a separate Sikh state. Nor is Sikh–Hindu hostility the only religious conflict in India. In the state of Gujerat, on India's west coast, tension between Hindus and Muslims in the 1980s has caused riot and massacre.

Religious divisions may be the basis of conflict in that they define who are the contending parties. The motives behind the conflict may be more complicated. Not everyone takes part in rioting or approves of it. Those who instigate violence may be highly strung personalities or even psychopaths, but many ordinary people take part. In situations of collective excitement, humans are capable of acting as members of a crowd in ways that they could not act were they on their own. It should also be remembered that political or economic interests may lie behind the formation of groups identified by religion. In Northern Ireland, for example, the contending parties are often identified as Protestant and Catholic, but the more fundamental opposition is that between the Unionists who want to keep the province part of the United Kingdom and the Republicans who want a united Ireland. Religious differences can also give a special character to conflicts defined in political terms, like the long war between Iran and Iraq. The Iranians and Iraqis follow different traditions within Islam and many of the states which support Iraq are influenced by their fear of the revolutionary potential of the Iranian tradition.

The UN Convention on Genocide was not drafted so as to bring the mass murder of political groups within its scope. The social processes which lead up to such murders are, however, basically similar to those underlying genocide. A strong sense of 'us' and 'them' is so manipulated as to make it possible for people to treat others in ways they would not treat those with whom they identify as members of a 'we' group. In Stalinist Russia whole national groups were deported. Khrushchev, in his denunciation of Stalin in 1956, referred to such actions as 'not dictated by any military consideration'. 'Not only a Marxist-Leninist', he declared, 'but also no man of common sense can grasp how it is possible to make whole nations responsible for inimical activity, including women, children, old people, Communists and Komsomols, to use mass represssion against them, and to expose them to misery and suffering for the hostile acts of individual persons or groups of persons.' In 1965, in Indonesia, there was a massacre of communists, mostly Chinese, on a massive scale. Estimates of the numbers slaughtered range from 200,000 to over 1 million. In Cambodia (or Democratic Kampuchea as it is currently called) the Khmer Rouge revolutionary forces turned the country into an agricultural work-site between 1974 and 1979, with the loss of possibly 2 million lives. The Pol Pot regime was then overthrown by an invading Vietnamese army. The UN still recognizes the successors of the Pol Pot regime as the legitimate government because some of the Great Powers do not wish to recognize the Vietnamese-supported regime in its place. The government of Idi Amin in Uganda from 1971 to 1979 practised political massacre on an almost comparable scale.

Linguistic differences rarely become a basis for such violent opposition as racial, religious, and political cleavages, but they can evoke powerful reactions when they serve to differentiate groups with opposed interests. In Quebec, French-speaking Canadians have referred to themselves as the country's 'white niggers'. The opposition between French-speakers and Flemish-speakers has brought down several governments of Belgium. Language differences have posed major political problems in Switzerland, and, closer home, in Wales. India has been forced by the strength of linguistic feeling to alter the boundaries of some of her states and in three instances to create new ones by dividing old states along linguistic boundaries.

All these kinds of opposition can have the effect, discussed in Chapter 3, of reducing harmony, increasing tension, and, at times, pushing the state either to breakdown, or, after a paroxsym of violence, of re-establishing harmonious relations dependent upon a new balance of power. Racial differences can occasion a particularly sharp divide, but they differ from the other sorts in degree rather than kind. What is fundamental is the process of polarization. Ties between the opposed groups are reduced. People are forced to align themselves with one side or the other and no intermediate positions are tolerated. Tensions grow until each group wishes to have a life of its own in which the others will have no part. If they stand in the way of this objective, they must be expelled or eliminated.

One of the principles upon which United Nations action has been founded is that of self-determination. The accession to independence of a large number of previously dependent territories has fashioned the majority view about the circumstances in which this principle is applicable. Since many new states have experienced salt-water imperialism, they contend that it is colonies such as they were which are entitled to self-determination. They deny its application to groups like the Falkland Islanders and the Gibraltarians. They assume that self-determination is fully realized when a colony achieves independence, and that it can be exercised only once by a popular majority at that time. Thus Burundi now has a government apparatus dominated by Tutsi. Any Hutu claims to self-determination would get little support in the Organization of African Unity or the UN. Both of those bodies are organizations of states rather than of nations. The rulers of one state are reluctant to interfere in the affairs of another, even when there are gross violations of human rights, lest by so doing they give other states a justification for interfering in what they see as their own affairs.

From a sociological standpoint, however, the kinds of conflict which arise within independent states, as groups struggle for power over others or for self-determination, may be little different from the struggles that hastened independence. In Nigeria large numbers of

59

energetic and talented people from the Eastern Region moved to work in the North, making a significant contribution to the economic and social development of the places to which they moved. Their relative success aroused resentment, and in 1966 getting on for 30,000 of them were massacred. Those who could, returned to the Eastern Region which shortly afterwards declared its independence under the name of Biafra. There was a long war which led to the death of between 600,000 and 1 million Easterners, yet there was no independence for Biafra.

Compare this with Bangladesh. From its foundation in 1948 Pakistan was divided into two parts, separated from one another by over 1,500 kilometres (1,000 miles). They had been made a single state because in each section most of the people were Muslims. West Pakistan was composed of the Baluchi, Pathan, Punjabi, and Sindhi peoples with Urdu as their common language. East Pakistan, composed predominantly of Bengali-speaking people, had a very different culture, geography, and economy. In 1948 the income *per caput* of people in the West was 10 per cent higher than that of people in the East. This disparity increased steadily until by 1969 there was a 60 per cent gap. The bulk of Pakistan's foreign exchange was earned in the East, but most of the foreign aid went to the West. The senior military personnel, the senior civil servants, the central government apparatus as a whole, were overwhelmingly West Pakistani. Many Easterners maintained that they were subject to colonial domination by Westerners. In 1970 the then military ruler, a Westerner, promised elections and constitutional changes which would have given the East a fairer deal. The Awami League campaigned in the East for the maximum autonomy short of separation. It won 167 out of the 169 seats allocated to East Pakistan in the National Assembly. The first meeting of that body was postponed while, apparently, negotiations were undertaken. In reality, the government used the delay to mobilize its military might. In March 1971 it struck. The International Commission of Jurists described the outcome as:

> the indiscriminate killing of civilians, including women and children and the poorest and weakest members of the community; the attempt to drive out of the country a large part of the Hindu population; the arrest, torture and killing of Awami League activists, students, professional and business men and other potential leaders among the Bengalis; the raping of women; the destruction of villages and towns; and the looting of property. All this was done on a scale which is difficult to comprehend.

In December, after the intervention of the Indian army, the war ended.

Estimates of the numbers of Bengalis killed in what then became Bangladesh vary, but the total may have approached 3 million. Account should also be taken of the 10 million Hindus forced to take refuge in India; the attacks upon them probably come within the legal definition of genocide. At the UN (on which see Kuper 1985: 44–61) Pakistan accused elements within the Awami League of plotting secession with encouragement from India. The government had to act in order to prevent the state from being broken up. Pakistan expressed regret that the international community had done so little to restrain India from a course of conduct which violated 'the two most fundamental principles of the Charter of the United Nations – non-interference in internal matters, and refraining from the threat or use of force against the territorial integrity or political independence of any state'. The right of self-determination could not be extended to an area that was an integral part of a state's territory for 'Pakistan is only one among the many multiracial, multi-linguistic or multi-religious states which would then be exposed to the dangers of fission and disintegration'. So the UN concentrated upon what it does so well: talking.

Thanks to India the people of Bangladesh were not denied self-determination, but the general pattern has been for states to channel ethnic sentiments to support state structures. In the days of decolonization African leaders promised that once they were independent they would be able to revise state boundaries to harmonize with ethnic boundaries. With the exception of Cameroon, no such revision has occurred. The pressures on the new leaders have been those of trying to hold together political entities dependent upon only flickering sentiments of national unity.

CONSTITUTIONAL LAW

Political leaders are frequently in a position to change a country's constitution so as to promote national integration, to secure a privileged position for their own group, or to provide a system of representation that recognizes ethnic differences. Clare Palley (1974) describes these three as assimilationist approaches, domination devices, and pluralistic techniques. In the first are counted measures to eliminate discrimination, such as special laws, Bills of rights, supervisory commissions, and bodies charged to enforce legislation, conciliate parties in dispute, monitor appointments, and so on. In the second come various manipulations of the electoral process, by making it more difficult for certain kinds of people to vote, varying the size of constituencies, and drawing the boundaries to favour one group ('gerrymandering'). In Malaysia, Civil Service posts are awarded disproportionately to Malay applicants. In the award of business licences and government contracts preference is shown to Malays or to partnerships between Malay and Chinese entrepreneurs. The law has been used to enforce the grossly unequal ownership of land by a dominant minority, as in South Africa and the former Southern Rhodesia, but it has also, on occasion, been utilized to protect indigenous groups (e.g. Maoris in New Zealand, Melanesians in Fiji, Indian reservations in the United States). Regulations concerning the use of an official language may be seen as a form of domination. National holidays, the national flag, and national dress may reflect only the traditions of the majority group.

Pluralist policies are varied. They include federal constitutions, territorial devolution, and arrangements to see that the number of elected representatives is in a fixed ratio. There may be separate electoral rolls for the different ethnic groups or a fixed distribution of important offices. The danger of formal communalism is that it reinforces the lines of ethnic differentiation and reduces the occasions for people to interact with members of other groups. Separate electoral rolls with separate blocs of seats have been tried in Fiji, Rhodesia, South Africa, British East Africa, Cyprus, India (for the benefit of the tribal peoples and so-called untouchable castes) and New Zealand (for the benefit of Maoris). Sometimes separate rolls have been maintained with voters allowed to vote for candidates on other lists so as to build up political support across ethnic lines. In Mauritius the population is divided into four categories: Hindu, Muslim, Sino-Mauritian, and General (i.e. Afro-Creole, Coloured, mestizo and white) each of which returns two Members of Parliament, and then a further eight are chosen as 'best losers' in proportion to the state of the parties but on the basis of representing any under-represented community. The system produces a House of sixty Members which reflects the population mix. In Bermuda, with a population divided almost equally between black and white, each constituency elects two Members, and this enables a party to nominate one black and one white candidate. Where communal representation exists, it may be supported by the requirement that this representation can be amended only with the support of each set of representatives or with a majority of two-thirds or even three-quarters of the legislature. There may be special provisions to ensure power-sharing. For example, the Cyprus constitution of 1960 required a 7:3 ratio of Greek to Turkish ministers. In Northern Ireland a scheme was introduced, unsuccessfully, for elections using a single transferable vote to be followed by the Secretary of State's appointing an executive to include Protestant and Catholic members from several political parties. The Lebanese National Pact of 1943–75 required that the President be a Maronite Christian, the Prime Minister a Sunni Muslim, and the Chairman of Parliament a Shi'ite. Only in Switzerland has power-sharing developed organically over a century. There a federal assembly elects a federal council of seven, such that there are usually four or five German-speakers, one or two French-speakers, and one Italian-speaker. This has promoted relatively good intercommunal relations.

Constitutional devices of this kind will be of crucial importance when there is a change of regime in South Africa. What would be disastrous for that country would be the adoption of single-Member constituencies with first-past-the-post elections on the British model. In ethnically divided societies, that model enables the largest group to dominate the others. The Nigerians recognized this some years ago and introduced a scheme which requires a candidate for the presidency to win votes in all eighteen states. The new rulers of South Africa will need to examine electoral systems in which voters will have to list candidates in order of preference in multi-Member constituencies. In this way it may be possible to build inter-ethnic coalitions and promote fluidity in party alignments.

Many attempts to promote harmonious group relations by constitutional measures have not brought the results hoped for. Much may depend upon economic circumstances. When there is no economic growth one group can gain only at another's expense so there is a zero-sum conflict in which the losing group is very resentful. This can develop into a cleavage, as, for example, in the expulsion of Asians from East Africa. When there is economic growth, one group can advance without the other's losing thereby. It is probable, for example, that there has been no further Malay–Chinese rioting in Malaysia since 1969 because that country's continuing economic growth has supported the preferential policies in the Malay interest without thereby reducing the economic level of the Chinese group. The positive-sum result is not because the internal conflict has been constructive but because the terms of trade have moved in Malaysia's favour and new sources of mineral wealth have been discovered.

The conclusion of this chapter must surely be that it is impossible to construct any meaningful scale of group harmony and group conflict because so much depends upon the particular characteristics and circumstances of the groups in contact. Nor is it easy to derive sociological generalizations when so much depends upon political relations that may change with great rapidity. The international order recognizes the legitimacy of state power rather than the rights of nations because it is difficult to take account of nations and national consciousness except in their expression through state institutions. Where there are national, ethnic, or racial divisions within states relative harmony and conflict depends upon competition to control state institutions and the use that is made of that control. Some generalizations about such use are advanced in Chapter 5.

CHAPTER 5

Increasing racial consciousness

White people in the United States and South Africa have attempted to reinforce their position of privilege in relation to black people in a more systematic way than that employed by the Tutsi in Burundi. To this end they have cultivated white racial consciousness by supporting doctrines of permanent differences in the capacities of races, for if there were any such differences there would be less scope for modifying racial relations by political action. Their measures have at the same time, and inadvertently, led to a growth of racial consciousness among the subordinated group or groups. The subordinated peoples have come to believe themselves oppressed and have created a wider political unity in opposition to their oppressors. A good way of uncovering the dynamism of racial relations is to consider five steps that might appeal to any government which wanted to construct a caste-like society in which racial inequality was unchallenged.

RACIAL CLASSIFICATION

The first step would be to establish a comprehensive system of racial classification. If some people are to enjoy special privileges and others to have lesser rights, there must be a systematic classification which makes clear who is entitled to what. Societies in which privilege is based upon race need no such system to classify people of wholly European descent as white and wholly African descent as black. They do need a system, however, for determining the status of people of mixed descent and people from regions in other parts of the world that do not fit into a European–African division.

When they first settled in the United States, people from England described themselves as English, as Christians, and as free; not until the end of that century did they start calling themselves white. From the Spanish language they borrowed the names Indian and Negro. In the eighteenth century they referred to Negroes as blacks and as Africans, but scarcely ever called them heathens or pagans. The child of a black–white union was called a mulatto. By 1705 a mulatto was defined in law as 'the child, grandchild or great-grandchild of a negro'. This meant that people of one-quarter or one-eighth African origin were assigned to the same category as people of entirely African origin. However, it is likely that, whatever the legal position, in everyday life some distinctions were drawn on the basis of shades of colour. There were parts of the United States where distinct communities of people of mixed origin formed (most notably in New Orleans after the purchase of Louisiana from the French in 1803).

In South Carolina also there was a significant mulatto class and the courts were unwilling to regard its members as of the same status as the blacks. Especially in Louisiana the terms quadroon, octoroon, and mustee were used to denote persons of mixed origin. Then from the late eighteenth century there was a boom in cotton production; the importation of slaves was stopped, so those already in the country became more valuable. As the number of coffee-coloured persons whether free or unfree grew, and with the existence of a class of free 'persons of colour' who in their cultural attributes were superior to many poor whites, there were forces operating to blur the colour line. But the free mulattos and blacks could not secure the intermediate positions in the economic structure because of the hostility of the well-to-do whites and the continuing influx of workers from Europe who wanted the artisan-style jobs for themselves. The slave-owners feared that the free mulattos and blacks threatened the slave order. The white workers saw them as competitors for jobs and benefits. As the white workers secured the vote, they used their power to restrain black competition, and so there was never any room for a mulatto escape hatch. The names for persons of mixed origin dropped out of use as the system polarized.

At the time of the American Revolution in 1776, the gradual emancipation of slaves seemed possible, but the growing demand for cotton and North-South tensions made the Southern states commit themselves to the slave order. Slavery was effectively ended by the defeat of the Southern army, and legally ended by the thirteenth amendment to the federal constitution. The period from 1865 to 1876 is called that of Reconstruction, as the federal government then attempted to reconstruct the Southern political order on a more equal basis. Its success was limited, for the new social order reasserted racial inequality, basing it upon custom and informal understandings instead of upon legal status. This new order is often called 'colour-caste' because it denied any possibility of mobility from the one stratum to the other, unlike systems of social class.

Colour-caste continued the form of racial classification which had been created under slavery. Anyone with any ascertainable degree of African descent was considered Negro (or black). This practice spread to the rest of the United States. Persons influenced by the culture of that country, as most Westerners now are, believe this classification to be natural when it is nothing of the sort. The contrast with other parts of the continent was highlighted by James Bryce when he wrote (in 1912) that 'In the United States everyone who is not white is classed as coloured, however slight the trace. In Spanish America everyone who is not wholly Indian is classed as white, however marked the Indian type.' It was repeated in more recent times in a story about a United States journalist who interviewed the President of Haiti. He asked what proportion of the island's population was white. The President replied, 'Oh, about 95 per cent.' The journalist was puzzled and enquired 'How do you define white?' The President responded by asking 'How do you define coloured?' The American said 'Well, anyone with Negro blood is coloured.' Said the President: 'Yes, that's our definition too, anyone with white blood is white.' This is an imaginary tale but it helps teach the lesson that if there are only two categories and people of intermediate appearance have to be assigned to one or other, they do not have to be assigned to the lower one. When they are, it is because the people in the upper category want to limit the numbers who share their privileges.

There were others besides blacks and whites who had to be found places. There were significant numbers of Native Americans (as American Indians are now called) living in the South. How were they to be counted? If they travelled on the railways, for example, were they to use the white or the black carriages and waiting-rooms? What about the Chinese who settled in Mississippi in the latter part of the nineteenth century? Such questions were settled not by doctrinal argument but by practical, everyday solutions. In Mississippi Native Americans were counted as black in those parts of the state where they were numerous, but not in areas where few of them were to be seen. Thus a Choctaw Indian could change his racial status by travelling 60 kilometres (40 miles). The Chinese had been brought to the state around 1870 as contract labourers. Some stayed after the expiry of their contracts and a small Chinese community was established. To start with its members were counted socially as black, but in areas where their numbers were sufficient separate schools were built. By the late 1930s more white schools were willing to admit Chinese pupils. They were the more welcome in those towns where whites were a minority relative to blacks and where, perhaps, the schools had difficulty recruiting enough pupils. As they prospered economically, the Chinese came to count as white.

Racial classification has been used to defend privilege. In Nazi Germany it was used to despoil and isolate a scapegoat group. A law was issued that 'A Jew is anyone who is descended from at least three grandparents who are racially full Jews. A Jew is also one who is descended from two full Jewish parents if (a) he belonged to the Jewish community at the time this law was issued . . .; or (b) was married to a Jewish person; or (c) was the offspring of a union between Jews.' The law stated: 'A Jew cannot be a citizen of the Reich. He has no right to vote in political affairs and he cannot occupy public office.' After the Nazis took power in Austria these laws were applied there. Someone who wished to demonstrate that he was an Aryan had to produce the baptismal certificates of all four grandparents. A friend of the author has described how he shared a school desk in Austria with a boy whose grandparents had all converted to Christianity. Therefore he counted as an Aryan but his parents, who were Christians, were legally 'full Jews'. His parents both perished in the extermination camp at Auschwitz while the son was conscripted at 16 years and died on the Russian front in a uniform several sizes too large for him, defending the values of his *Vaterland*.

Consciousness of racial differences in South Africa has undergone important changes over the centuries, particularly in the interior. A study of the parentage and marriages of the Afrikaans-speaking whites showed that in 1807 at least a quarter (and if unions outside marriage be included, up to a third) of that population had a black or brown grandparent. Today, on average 7 per cent of the Afrikaners' genetic inheritance is from black Africans (Afrikaners are the descendants of Dutch settlers; they have often been referred to as Boers, *boer* being the Dutch word for farmer). In the first half of the nineteenth century settlers living in the interior, and herding sheep and goats, dressed themselves in skins from their own animals. They had adapted to their environment. On the frontier the whites needed to co-operate with the native people. Whites were not all masters; non-whites were not all servants. The big change came in the last quarter of the century as a result of the discovery first of gold and then of diamonds. The rapid development of mining brought new capital investment and attracted fortune-hunters; it transformed the basis of social and political life. South Africa was at this time a British colony. The Afrikaners attempted to establish independent republics, free of British rule. This resulted in what the British saw as a rebellion, and they crushed it with great loss of life by the South African War of 1899–1902. Afterwards the British promoted co-operation between the English-speaking and the Afrikaans-speaking whites, and made concessions to the latter with this in view. In 1910 the country acquired a degree of independence as a dominion within the Commonwealth under the name Union of South Africa.

In the period following the war, any reference to racial relations in South Africa was likely to relate to what were thought of as two white races distinguished by language, by two forms of the Protestant religion, by history and culture, but not by appearance. The Afrikaners saw themselves as a *volk* (a people) or a *nasie* (nation); they saw the various African groups, Zulu, Xhosa, Swazi, etc., likewise as peoples or nations. The Afrikaners had, and have, a high consciousness of membership in their own group, and of white solidarity (as incorporating the English-speaking whites). They do not readily think of themselves, or refer to themselves as a race unless they have been influenced by the way people in Europe and North America apply this word. Nor do the other whites, the Indians, the Cape Coloured, or the African ethnic groups necessarily think of themselves as races. The Cape Coloured people (who are of partly African and partly European origin) mostly speak Afrikaans. It is interesting that by 1977 more than half the Afrikaners questioned in surveys should have said that they would call an Afrikaans-speaking Coloured an Afrikaner. Chapter 1 maintained that ethnic and racial groups are composed by sets of people who can be distinguished on several dimensions, by shared history, appearance, religion, language, etc. The relative importance of criteria may change over the years and the groups that in different countries are called racial are not differentiated in quite the same ways. So it is important not to assume that 'race' in South Africa denotes the same kinds of difference and the same sorts of feeling as it does in some other country.

South Africa provides another example of an imperial power transferring power to a dominant ethnic group. The political dynamic behind the policies of the white parties during the first half-century of independence was the white workers' fear of competition from black labour. Most of the poor whites were Afrikaners forced off the land to seek a living in the towns and at the mines. They demanded a privileged position in the labour market and found their champions in the National Party which was voted into office in 1948 and immediately set about implementing its dream of apartheid or separateness. The period from 1948 to the assassination of Prime Minister Hendrik Verwoerd in 1966 can be seen as one in which the politicians tried to create a social order resembling the colour-caste of the United States. It envisaged parallel white and black societies with the whites in control of the region. This plan could not be reconciled either with the pressures generated by a capitalist economic system or with the expectations of international opinion, so from about 1970 leaders of the National Party have been trying to find compromises. In the eyes of the world the changes have not been sufficient.

One of the first actions of the new Nationalist government in 1948 was the enactment of the Population Registration Act of 1950 which empowered the Director of Census to assign all persons to racial categories. Prior to that time people had been able to pass as members of a more privileged group if their physical features allowed it. Sometimes this brought a significant improvement in their social position, such as higher rates of pensions, greater freedom of movement, rights to reside in more attractive localities, send their children to better schools, and so on. The 1950 Act provided for a register, based in part on the census of 1910, which would classify every resident as White, Native or Coloured according to his or her appearance and how he or she was socially regarded. Nine years later the Coloured category was divided into seven subgroups so as to differentiate Cape Coloured, Cape Malay, Chinese, Indian, etc. Some whites who associated with non-whites found themselves classified as Coloured. Under the Registration Act persons were sometimes assigned to a category different from that to which they were allocated under the Group Areas Act, or the one for voting, or the one to which they had been assigned by the courts. An interdepartmental commission was appointed to formulate a uniform set of definitions for the purposes of all legislation, but in 1957 it reported that the task was beyond its powers. There were no objective criteria by which all persons of mixed ancestry could be classified. Therefore such classifications had to be arbitrary. Yet once they had been officially recorded it was extremely difficult for an individual to have his or her classification changed. Much depended upon these official records. For example a white person was unable to contract a lawful marriage with someone who was differently classified. The legal strengthening of the system of racial classification therefore did much to increase racial consciousness and tension (Kuper, 1960).

SEGREGATION

The second step to be taken by a government seeking to prevent change would be to ensure that racial classification was the basis for determining a person's entitlement in as wide a range of situations as possible. If some people enjoy special privileges and others have lesser rights, the rationale of the differentiation will be more difficult to enforce if a distinction is held relevant in one set of circumstances but not another. If blacks and whites are segregated on trains and buses they have to be segregated on aeroplanes too. By the end of the 1950s the following social situations were in South Africa regulated by laws based upon racial criteria: marriage; 'illicit carnal intercourse'; proximity between neighbours and traders; inclusion on a common electoral roll; school education for Africans; reservations of occupations; control of contact in trade; black–white contact in churches, schools, hospitals, clubs, places of entertainment, public assemblies, university education. In the Deep South of the United States there was at the end of the nineteenth and in the early decade of the twentieth century a similar trend which in 1930 led Birmingham, Alabama, to legislate against blacks and whites playing at dominoes or checkers together; while in 1935 Oklahoma separated the races while fishing or boating.

The trend towards comprehensive segregation has to contend with opposing pressures because it may be in the economic interest of individuals to base their relations on economic rather than racial criteria. In the Deep South this stretched into the white household. Many white children were brought up by black mammies and domestic servants. It was said that in Southern society the black person could be very close to the whites but must not be allowed to get any higher. In Northern society the racial communities were physically and socially separate; the black person could climb high in the economic scale but never came any closer to the whites. The Southern system operated by exempting from many of the requirements of segregation any situation in which the white person established a personal relation with the black person. This was a kind of safety-valve which could enable people to get round the rigid application of the principle of segregation. That principle depended upon each party knowing the racial classification of the other party. In an agricultural society like that of the South in the early decades of the twentieth century this posed few problems, but the position changed with urbanization and technological developments like the motor car and the telephone. The rules of the road could not be based

71

upon the racial status of the drivers. It could be difficult to guess whether the person at the other end of the telephone was black or white. New structures working on bureaucratic principles became increasingly important. The implementation of their rules was sometimes distorted by the belief that blacks were not entitled to equal treatment, but in the United States these were distortions of a formally egalitarian structure. In South Africa racial classification was reinforced by the new bureaucratic structures. They made it impossible for people to enter into social relations until the status of the other party was known because that determined the kind of behaviour thought appropriate. Cases have been reported of black people who died after accidents because no ambulances for black people were available to take them to hospital. White ambulances were available but could not be used.

SANCTIONS

A third step to hinder change would be needed to deal with those in either the superordinate or the subordinate group who broke the rules. In a racially divided society people on either side of the divide will exploit the rules about classification when it suits them and try to get round them when they run counter to their interests. For example, if a colour bar confines black workers to unskilled occupations this is likely to increase the supply of unskilled labour. A colour bar will then be in the interest of those employers (like mine-owners and farmers) whose businesses require much unskilled labour; it may be against the interest of employers of skilled labour, who may as a result have to negotiate with white trade unions exercising monopoly powers over the supply of scarce skilled labour. Employers of skilled labour who find black workers able to perform the work they want carried out, may create new job categories which are not classed as skilled labour even if the distinction is artificial. Since the employers will not need to pay workers in these new categories the same wages as are paid to skilled workers, it is very much to their advantage to get round the rules in this way. The government may have difficulty stopping them.

If inequality is to be enforced there must be sanctions to reward the obedient and punish the disobedient. The informal pressures of life in small communities may generate sanctions that are more effective than a government's rules. More than three and a half centuries ago,

Francis Bacon wrote that 'he that hath wife and children hath given hostages to fortune'. The force of this observation was exemplified in the Deep South, for a white man who failed to observe local norms of racial propriety in his dealings with blacks, would find that his wife and children suffered on his account. With social and economic life based upon relatively small communities and a slowly changing technology, there were real risks for the person who attracted social disapproval. When, in the 1960s, the 'freedom riders' rode into Southern towns on interstate coach services to enforce the desegregation of those services, they were met by white vigilantes who assaulted both white and black. When civil rights activists campaigned in the Deep South to get more blacks on electoral rolls, white workers as well as blacks were murdered. But the considerable force mustered by white supremacists could not prevail against the power of the federal government supported by public opinion across the continent. By enforcing new civil rights laws the President, the Congress and the judiciary carried through what has been called a 'second Reconstruction', enabling black Americans to acquire a political influence more nearly proportionate to their numbers. For them this was the fulfilment of the transfer of power nearly two centuries before.

In South Africa the Nationalist government acted quickly against the threat to its policies posed by dissident whites. In 1950 it introduced the Suppression of Communism Act based upon a loose but comprehensive definition of communism. That government always chose nice-sounding names for repressive legislation, just as one of the more unpleasant Nazi laws was entitled the Law for the Protection of German Blood and German Honour. The South African definition of communism included 'the encouragement of feelings of hostility between the European and non-European races' if the consequences of such hostility was to 'bring any political, industrial, social or economic change'. So if the government passed a law that, because it was discriminatory, caused racial hostility, this was not 'communism'; but it was 'communism' if anyone protested against it in a manner which caused disorder. By this Act the Minister was empowered to name as a communist anyone who had ever 'advocated, advised, defended or encouraged the achievement of any of the objects of communism' either actively or by any 'omission which is calculated to further the achievement of any such object'. If someone was named as a communist it became impossible for him or her to engage in normal political activity. This was a powerful weapon against dissent within the white population, but by identifying communism with opposition to government policies it may have attracted some people to communism. The more recent introduction of far-reaching powers to censor the reporting of unrest in the mass media further illustrates the principle that the preservation of racial inequality means less freedom for both blacks and whites.

GROUP COMPETITION

A fourth kind of step to hinder change has to be taken in the economic sphere. The individual's search for his or her own advantage is one of the major sources of social change and if this is not regulated it will undermine relations based upon racial rather than economic status. Consider the position of a white person with a house to sell in a middle-class white neighbourhood. Assume that blacks have hitherto lived mostly in working-class neighbourhoods because their incomes have been low, but that some blacks now have higher incomes and wish to live in the sorts of locality favoured by white people with similar incomes. If blacks have previously had difficulty moving into such areas, a property there will be more valuable to them than to a white purchaser whose chances are less constrained. The vendor of the house might therefore be offered, say, £100,000 by prospective white purchasers and £110,000 by prospective black purchasers. The vendor might prefer to sell to a white, but, unless some other factor intervenes, there must be some price at which he or she will sell to a black purchaser who offers more. If a sale goes through at, say, £115,000, the extra £15,000 represents the price that the vendor sets upon his or her preference to sell to a white. If vendors are free to act in this way there will gradually be a reduction in racial segregation in residence. There will be similar effects in the employment market and in other areas of economic activity. So a government which wants to prevent such change will pass laws to prevent people acting in accordance with their individual interest if this disregards the racial status of the parties. It will seek to channel the search for economic advantage in directions which strengthen the racial order instead of weakening it.

The general proposition is that when people compete as individuals this tends to dissolve the boundaries that define racial groups; when they compete as groups this reinforces those boundaries. In an open housing market, properties will be sold to the highest bidder because, over time, preferences for sale to purchasers of similar race will diminish. But if the market is divided up, with some houses being for whites only and some for blacks only, some people will suffer because of restrictions upon the alternatives open to them. Others will be anxious to defend their privileges. These forces will make them more conscious of racial differences and more inclined to organize as groups either to defend the prevailing order or to overturn it.

Group competition can be seen with greatest clarity where racial groups lay claim to particular occupations and prevent members of other groups obtaining employment in those occupations. The study *Deep South*, conducted in a Mississippi town in the early 1930s (Davis *et al.* 1941: 424–8), reported that blacks could not secure employment as clerks, bookkeepers, or secretaries in white businesses, but only as porters, messengers, janitors, or maids. In automobile repair shops they were not given the status of mechanics. In one instance where a Negro worked as a mechanic he was paid a lower wage and was given additional duties of a menial kind. Skilled and mechanical work was reserved for whites but there were circumstances (e.g. in businesses not in local ownership) in which Negroes did skilled work but were paid less than whites. White workers were not supposed to accept unskilled employment in what were considered 'Negro jobs'. During the depression years of 1930–35, this changed because unemployed white workers wanted the 'Negro jobs'. The employers preferred the black workers because they worked harder and were more obedient, but the white workers had the political influence which enabled them to force blacks out of municipal employment as street-cleaners and garbage collectors. They took over the labouring work on construction sites. On the railways ten black firemen were shot, six fatally, by whites who wanted them to resign their posts. The firemen were members of a union and since other black members of that union were willing to take the places of those who had been shot, the black workers were able to repulse the attempted take-over. The incident shows, however, that the inter racial struggle in the job market was fierce.

In South Africa the white workers' claims to the skilled positions were enforced by law. In 1904 when the mine-owners were desperate for labour, the government arranged for the importation of over 50,000 Chinese labourers on contract. To mitigate protest from white workers a schedule was compiled of jobs from which the Chinese would be barred, and this list subsequently became a basis for excluding blacks from the same posts. The principle was then extended, by legislation, from mining to agriculture, manufacturing, transport, public administration, and professional work; in this last-named, exceptions were made only to allow for non-Europeans to serve as teachers and ministers of religion for their own groups. In the years following the Nationalist Party's victory in 1948 these laws were extended. For example, the Nursing Act of 1957 laid down that the Nursing Council, which dealt with the registration, training and discipline of nurses and midwives, was to consist of white persons only. It was to keep separate registers for nurses and midwives of the separate races, and was empowered to prescribe different qualifications for registration and different uniforms and badges. No white nurse might be employed under the control or supervision of any non-white nurse. One of the impulses behind government policy from the 1920s onwards was the desire to help poor white Afrikaner workers forced out of agriculture into urban employment. The Nationalists objected to the idea that white workers should have to compete for jobs with black workers. Job reservations enabled the poor whites to acquire a middle-class life-style. By the end of the 1950s this objective had been achieved and the Afrikaans-speaking whites were starting to catch up on the English-speaking whites. After 1970 the ideological impulse behind government policy weakened. Employers were allowed to upgrade black labour if they could do this without evoking protest from white workers. Non-Europeans were allowed to form trade unions. The rules regarding racial segregation at work were eased or abolished.

When social relations are regulated by law in such detail as has been employed in South Africa, a large bureaucracy is needed to administer the laws. In South Africa that bureaucracy has been staffed primarily by Afrikaans-speaking whites, though a substantial proportion of police are now black. People employed to administer a structure of this kind have an interest in preserving that structure, and in South Africa they have been able to prevent some projected reforms. Government policy regarding employment, as in other areas, has created clear racial categories; people have been obliged to compete as group members opposed to men and women who are members of other groups; this has reinforced the racial boundaries and increased tension. Yet there remain major tensions and differences of opinion within the racial categories. The whites are divided about the political policies appropriate to their current position. The non-whites are divided in their assessments of the political prospects, in their ethnic allegiances, and in the concern of the various socio-economic groups to preserve their gains relative to other groups. The government has had some success in channelling the search for individual advantage so as to make non-whites concentrate their attention upon possible short-term gains relative to other non-whites, and in this way deflecting their attention from bigger inequalities.

TRANSMITTED INEQUALITY

The fifth step to be taken by a government seeking to preserve political order based upon racial inequality, is of a negative kind. It is to permit and encourage the tendencies for socio-economic inequalities to be transmitted from one generation to the next. These tendencies exist in all societies except the very simplest, so no government has to create them. It can increase them or it can reduce their effect by taxing the inheritance of property and wealth, by promoting equal opportunity in education, and so on. It cannot prevent some parents giving their children a better start in life than other parents can. One of the reasons why people respond to the incentive of higher pay for more difficult work, or for working longer hours, is that they want to give their children extra benefits. It is not in the interest of any economic system to try to combat so important a motivation to work, but many societies do seek to limit the extent to which this motivation restricts equality of opportunity in the next generation.

In any racially divided society racial inequalities will be transmitted from one generation to the next. Where there are distinct racial groups with differential privileges like the Deep South and South Africa, group membership will be transmitted. In many other societies, including Great Britain, the associations between group membership and socio-economic status will be of a statistical character. There may be proportionately fewer blacks in the upper classes and proportionately more in the lower classes. As a result there may well be an image of blacks as lower-class people and this image will work to the detriment of all blacks. It will be strengthened by the psychological phenomenon of stereotyping. The process by which an unfavourable image comes about will be considered in Chapter 6 in connection with statistical discrimination. For present purposes, the argument is that in most societies unequal achievement in one generation has consequences for the next generation. If whites do better than blacks in the first generation, white children in the next generation will have an advantage, but the extent of the advantage will vary from one family to another. The children of high-achieving black parents will have a greater advantage than the children of low-achieving white parents. No individual will be privileged or handicapped because of his or her colour, and there will be no point at which discrimination occurs. At the same time there will be an association between an individual's skin colour and his or her chances in life. A government which takes no action to reduce that association will be able to maintain a racially unequal social order. It will be able to defend its inactivity by arguing that inequality between groups results from differences in the natural abilities of individuals, just as inequalities within groups result from individual differences.

Five steps have been outlined: (i) classify racially; (ii) segregate; (iii) introduce sanctions; (iv) channel group competition; (v) permit the transmission of inequality. A government which succeeded in implementing them could follow a policy of 'divide and rule' and persuade its subjects that the resulting inequalities were natural rather than social. For many centuries people all over the globe have accepted positions of inferiority as no more than their due. In Rwanda and Burundi the structure of inequality was facilitated by the belief of the Tutsi in their superiority and the acquiescence of the Hutu. It has often taken generations for a genuinely political consciousness to emerge among subordinated peoples, but the pace of change has been speeded up in the late twentieth century. Contact with other peoples prompts the revision of inherited expectations. The media of mass communication flash new assumptions and new images around the world. As noted in Chapter 4, elections were a catalyst stimulating the Hutu to believe that their votes were worth as much as the votes of their traditional masters. The extension of the suffrage, and the basis on which it has been granted, has everywhere been full of significance for racial relations.

Ruling groups usually seek to divide their opponents, but political tensions within their groups often limit the extent to which they do so. In the United States plantation system a distinction was drawn between house slaves and field slaves. There was a small population of free blacks, mainly in the towns. A superordinate group which set out systematically to preserve its privileges would have cultivated such divisions. When the suffrage was extended it would have used a property qualification to create an alliance with the richer blacks and check the aspirations of the poorer whites. Over-confident, unable to take a longer view, and solicitous of poor white support, leaders of the whites saw no need for such policies. The same comment applies with at least equal force to South Africa. At the beginning of this century qualified male members of the Coloured population of the Cape province could vote in parliamentary elections. From 1910 they were allowed to vote only for whites who would represent them. Proposals by Afrikaner political leaders to allow additional privileges to the Coloured and Indian groups, building them up as buffers between the blacks and whites, never received much support from white voters. The strength of the rural Afrikaner vote and the nature of the political forces within the white group have dictated the drawing of a boundary around white privilege.

In South Africa policies of divide and rule have been intertwined with the Afrikaners' conception of nationality. They survived as a *volk* although the might of the British Empire was deployed against them. They recognize the possibility that African ethnic groups may demonstrate a comparable national spirit. Since 1959 it has been government policy to preserve the main ethnic divisions within the African population and count the blacks as citizens of ten national states. Between 1976 and 1982 four of these (Transkei, Bophuthatswana, Venda, Ciskei) were declared independent sovereign states able to send out their own diplomatic, sporting, and other representatives, just like any other states. The governments of every other country in the world have refused to recognize these 'Bantustans' as independent, regarding them as puppets created to serve the political and economic convenience of the whites. The other six 'national states' still within the Republic have declined to follow their example. All the plans for racial segregation are thwarted by the white economy's demand for a massive black labour force in and around the cities. Of the 26.5 million people in South Africa in 1980, the 'Bantustans' and 'national states' accounted for only 9.5 million; all the rest were in so-called 'white areas' – 4.3 million whites, 2.5 million coloureds, 0.8 million Asians, and 9.5 million blacks. The black population is growing rapidly. According to a conservative projection it may have increased from 19 to 46 million by the year 2023. The recent official study, *Demographic Trends in South Africa*, analyses the trends in the 'black' and the 'nonblack' population, reflecting the desire of some whites to shift the line along which the major division is drawn.

When governments have introduced and enforced laws which preserve racial inequalities they may not have been working consciously from a blueprint designed to create a new kind of caste system, or one intended to promote racial consciousness or social tension. The actions of governments are usually impelled by a

79

mixture of motives among their members and those whose votes they want to attract. In South Africa National Party leaders had such a blueprint, but usually policies have reflected what seemed expedient at the time. If, however, a government did wish to preserve a racially unequal political order and sought sociological advice about how to do it, that advice would have to recommend the five steps just described. If a government wanted to implement policies of the opposite effect, the advice would be diametrically opposite.

The history of black–white relations in the United States and South Africa can be interpreted in terms of the equilibrium model represented in Fig. 3.3. To do so it is necessary to see the superordinate group (P) as internally divided (along class or ethnic lines, for example). The subordinate group (B) may also be divided. The effect of the P group's divisions will be considered first. In the United States the whites established themselves as the superordinate group in the cotton-growing South. Under the slave regime the white upper class set about building a paternalistic social order which (with exceptions) encouraged the establishment of settled slave communities with their own social hierarchies. Upper-class whites could be contemptuous of 'poor white trash'. The policies of their class were challenged in the course of the nineteenth century by non-slave-holding whites and immigrant white workers who demanded preferential treatment by comparison with blacks. Their demands for equality among whites added to the pressure for a sharp white–black split and for racial status to regulate all social contacts. It was, metaphorically speaking, their descendants who attacked the freedom riders in the 1960s. The system of colour-caste as it developed towards the end of the nineteenth century represented a new equilibrium in which the privileges of the poorer whites were protected by new methods. It was the outcome, not of planning, but of political struggles among the whites. In the South African P group the main division was between a commercially oriented English-speaking group and the rural Afrikaners. As events leading to the 1922 miners' strike suggested, the business class was prepared to relax the job colour bar. This kind of change was blocked by white workers, both Afrikaans- and English-speaking, who used their political power to increase their privileges relative to the voteless black workers. Their alliance with Afrikaner ideologists became the foundation of apartheid as a scheme for establishing a political equilibrium. Whereas the United States stumbled upon policies corresponding to the first four of the five steps mentioned, the National Party had them planned.

Since the second Reconstruction started in the mid 1960s, the United States has been seeking a new equilibrium. The old one had been upset because the Southern whites who would have wished to defend it no longer had sufficient power within a federal system affected by increased black pressure and the criticism of whites outside the South. Many people envisage the United States of the future as a country in which there will still be distinctive black and white groups but with a more equitable sharing of privileges. However, there is a sense in which processes of individual change, as exemplified in Fig. 3.2, are also important. Everyone in the United States, whatever their group membership, is increasingly influenced by the media of mass communication, by consumption patterns and economic trends which show little regard for group differences, and by the technology of communication, transport, etc., which shows none at all. So while racial classification remains, the range of its social relevance (the second of the five steps) is declining. So seen, the United States is passing round the circuit of Fig. 3.3 to an equilibrium in which black and white are roughly equal or the distinction has ceased to matter.

The situation in South Africa differs because there those who wish to defend white privilege at present control the entire state apparatus. The result of the 1987 whites-only election indicated that there is insufficient support within the existing electorate for any major alteration, so that changes will come from extra-parliamentary non-white opposition and from international pressures. Once again it is not only relations between the P and B groups which alter, but relations within them. It is therefore time to consider divisions with the subordinate group.

RESPONSES TO RACIAL SUBORDINATION

For this purpose it is better to consider relations among the blacks of South Africa before those among Afro-Americans, because black South Africans were an indigenous people who had to contend with an invasion from overseas. The blacks were divided along ethnic lines. Some, notably the Zulu, mobilized to attack the invaders but were eventually defeated on the battlefield. Most of the African groups were located in what since 1961 has been the Republic of South Africa, though some remained under British protection in what are now the independent states of Botswana, Lesotho, and

Swaziland. These states are economically dependent upon South Africa; their people have experienced a similar racial subordination and have been drawn into the growing sense of a common interest spanning all the non-white groups. While the Pretoria government's policy evokes and fashions this political consciousness, the state also has the means to restrain it. The head of the security service told a United States journalist (Lelyveld 1986: 331) that the African National Congress (ANC) was crippled by the knowledge that any effort it might make to recruit large numbers of blacks to its membership would increase the number of informers in their ranks. The President of the ANC confirmed that this was the case. Well-trained infiltrators were often not detected by their screening processes.

The powers of the state apparatus are so great that many of the chief advances in black political consciousness have resulted from miscalculations by those who exercised these powers. On 21 March 1960 a crowd of some 10,000 Africans gathered at Sharpeville to protest at the pass laws. The local detachment of white police panicked and fired into the crowd, killing 67 and injuring 186. R. W. Johnson (1977: 17) suggests that the event was in many ways comparable to the Russian Revolution of 1905. It took everyone by surprise, the government, the liberals, and the revolutionaries, just as when the police fired on the workers' rally in St Petersburg; it transformed the political scene. The ANC (no revolutionary organization) and the Pan-African Congress (which had split from it on the grounds that the ANC was dominated by white communists) were both banned. International pressure mounted so that South Africa left the Commonwealth and the Dutch Reformed Church of South Africa withdrew from the World Council of Churches. Overseas financiers took fright and investment faltered. As the government tightened its control the main anti-apartheid movements within the country either dissolved or went into exile. They lost touch with events in the black townships and gave up any influence they might have had in shaping political movements there.

On 17 May 1976 the pupils of a secondary school in Soweto (an African dormitory town for workers in Johannesburg) walked out. They said they would not return until a new rule that they should be taught in Afrikaans was withdrawn. Implementation of this rule was being pressed by a right-wing Afrikaner minister more concerned to win the favour of Afrikaner voters than to ascertain whether there was a realistic chance of making the schools toe this ideological line. Pupils in other Soweto schools left their classrooms and marched to the school where the strike had begun. Confronted by police armed with tear-gas and machine-guns, they attacked buildings and property associated with white authority. Rioting spread. The police refused to give any figures for the number of deaths resulting from the disturbances, but unofficial estimates put the total well above 1,000.

The late 1960s saw the beginnings of the Black Consciousness Movement which stressed the need for blacks to overcome any feelings of inferiority and to become more assertive without excluding Coloureds and Indians. Its most eloquent exponent was Steve Biko, the first President of the South African Students' Organization, who was brutalized and killed in 1977 while in police custody. When asked about Biko's death, the Minister of Police declared, 'It leaves me cold', a response which only added to the world-wide indignation about a government which permitted, and even encouraged, such action by its employees. There was subsequent criticism of the medical profession for not controlling more effectively the actions of doctors who certified the causes of prisoners' deaths and did not discipline doctors who helped the police conceal their own law-breaking. It says a great deal about the outlook prevailing in the government that it was so little concerned about world opinion.

Since 1984 the United Democratic Front has been the most influential black political organization within the country; it has resurrected the slogans and themes of the ANC, but it has won less support among the Zulu who look more to their own Chief Butelezi and to the *Inkatha* Movement. The Anzanian Peoples' Organization is most radical, apparently considering that the restitution of African land must be one of the priorities for the new government of Anzania, the name to be given to the successor state. However, now that black trade unions can operate legally (even if they cannot accumulate strike funds) and the National Union of Mineworkers has demonstrated its ability to muster support for a three-week strike, it may be that the growth of black industrial power will be the main internal source of political change. At present there seems little likelihood that groups outside South Africa can bring about major changes within the country. It would have greatly helped the country's economy had she been able to expand her trade with the black African states. That she has been unable to do, but it has also meant that she is the less vulnerable. The United Kingdom and the United States have been unwilling for economic and political reasons to join with the countries who wish to impose an economic blockade. So the precarious political equilibrium is preserved.

The response of Afro-Americans to racial subordination has been different, chiefly because they came to think of themselves as a people only in what was, to start with, an alien land. Without having had the opportunity to offer military resistance, they experienced something comparable to defeat followed by dispersal and exploitation. The men, women, and children who were for the most part sold by their fellow Africans, loaded onto the slave-ships, and transported to the Americas, came from a great variety of ethnic groups. Under the slave regime they resisted white prejudice as individuals and in small communities. Only rarely could they plan wider revolts and all those in the United States failed. After the Civil War of 1861–65 Afro-Americans remained economically and politically weak. The experience of white discrimination gave them a sense of being a people, though unlike other peoples they could not base their grouping upon ownership of a territory (the nearest parallel to their case is that of the Palestinians who, after losing territory consequent upon the creation of the state of Israel in 1948, have come to a new consciousness of being a people). Afro-Americans had to contend with the problems that beset conquered peoples, but experienced them in a more acute form than, say, the Germans after 1918 or 1945. The Germans could look back with pride upon a long sequence of historical and cultural achievements. Defeat was seen as only a set-back. Yet still it had momentous political consequences, contributing to the rise of Nazism in the interwar period and to an extremist strand of nationalism that is still a political threat.

The Afro-Americans' predicament was the more acute because they could not look back to such a history. Were they to see themselves as a people in captivity? Or were they immigrants, like the whites, and with as much right to be in a new land building a new society even if it was unable to live up to its professed ideals and left them at a temporary disadvantage? Were they primarily blacks or primarily Americans? They spoke the same language as the whites and, for the most part, embraced the same versions of Christianity as the white population. In resisting oppression they had drawn heavily upon the Christian message of human equality in the sight of God, so it was not surprising that a minority thought that in religion there were clues as to their special identity. By 1900 Negro preachers were travelling through the Carolinas teaching that Negroes were the lost sheep of the House of Israel. In 1913 a Moorish Science Temple was founded in Newark which taught that Afro-Americans were really Moors and Muslims. The first step towards true emancipation was for blacks to appreciate who they really were, and to assume their proper name. The Black Muslims grew into an important social and political movement in the 1960s. Its leader told his followers that they were not 'Negroes'; that this was only a label the white men had placed upon them to make discrimination easier. Entry into the movement was marked by the discarding of what was called a slave name (i.e. a surname which may have derived from some white slave-owner) and by rebirth into a new identity with a new first name followed by the letter X to denote both the change ('ex') and the mystery of destiny. Thus one of the most celebrated black leaders of the 1960s took the name Malcolm X. People who suffer racial discrimination are sometimes reluctant to acknowledge that others regard their group with scorn. Unless they have the emotional support of their fellows and an explanation of why prejudice should be directed against them, people may find it psychologically easier to assume that they have failed to progress because of their individual limitations than to face up to the strength of the forces ranged against them collectively. Many black people were unconsciously uncomfortable with their skin colour. To claim a new name could signify a recognition that the old identity was demeaned, a rejection of that identity, and the assumption of a new one. It could be a change comparable to a religious conversion.

In the United States up to the 1960s, 'coloured' was generally considered the best name for people with any degree of African ancestry, both by the people themselves and by others. Many of the people so designated had very light brown complexions and the word 'coloured' seemed suitable because it comprehended all the varying shades. At the time blackness was thought ugly and undesirable, so that to call someone black was to say something wounding. Coloured was a kinder description. In the United States the main alternative to coloured as a name was Negro, and this was preferred by some who thought it could be used with a greater sense of pride, as by the black nationalists who joined the Universal Negro Improvement Association. To start with, Negro was spelled without any capital letter. Since the names of national groups (e.g. Canadians) and Native American groups (e.g. Apache, Iroquois) were spelled with capitals, so it became a point of dignity to insist on a capital letter for Negro. The political movement for racial equality in the first half of the twentieth century organized round an attack on mistaken racial beliefs and their use to justify racial inequalities. The idea that people could be meaningfully divided into racial categories and that they should be treated according to their category membership rather than their individual merits, was vigorously denied. The categories should be dissolved.

Racial consciousness

All this was soon to change. One day in 1960 four black students sat at the lunch counter in a store in North Carolina and waited to be served. Within a month, thousands of black and white students 'sat in' at lunch counters throughout the South and began a wave of sit-ins, drive-ins, wade-ins, play-ins, kneel-ins, teach-ins, and so on, wherever services were segregated. Blacks seized the leadership of the Civil Rights Movement. They demanded that all people of African or partly African descent in the United States call themselves black and that others call them black. They adopted or adapted African hairstyles, items of African costume, and African names. They demanded black studies and the opportunity to learn African languages. Their slogans were the call for black power and the insistence that 'black is beautiful'. Their movement inspired a series of attempts at imitation by other minorities in the United States. It influenced the strategy of the women's movement in that country. It was imitated overseas, and in South Africa was referred to as the Black Consciousness Movement. Seen internationally, that is perhaps the best name for it.

If there was no more reason to be ashamed of a black colour than any other kind of colour, then it could no longer be hurtful to be called black. Afro-Americans outside the Civil Rights Movement were less inclined to change their self-definitions, so the activists suggested that those who called themselves coloured did so because they were frightened to call themselves black. Their message appealed to the younger generation and to city-dwellers. A measure of its spread is given by Table 5.1 showing the racial designations preferred by respondents of African descent in two surveys in Detroit. There had, for a long time, been groups of black people in the northern cities who thought that blacks should identify with Africa. They constituted a movement often called cultural nationalism for this reason. It would therefore have been interesting had the respondents been invited to choose between the three alternatives grouped together in the third line. Afro-American may well become more

Table 5.1   Racial designations preferred by blacks in Detroit

	1968	1971
Coloured	12	6
Negro	59	38
Black, or Afro-American, or black-American	23	53
Other	6	3

(*Source:* Aberbach and Walker 1970)

popular as a designation. Hyphenated names like Irish-American, Italian-American, and Polish-American have been current for a long time. Anglo-American is now being used more in place of WASP or 'White Anglo-Saxon Protestant'. To say Afro-American will therefore be consistent with the designation of other groups. It is possible, too, that the names for the minorities of European origin may slightly reduce the emotional associations with the adjective 'white', for the designation white is open to objections similar to those brought against black and coloured. It is inaccurate; it is value-laden; and it introduces a discontinuity into what is socially as well as physically a continuous distribution.

The Black Consciousness Movement in the United States attacked those forms of segregation which denied blacks access to public facilities, but it favoured self-segregation in the social sphere. On university campuses black students demanded all-black student houses (or 'dormitories'). Sometimes they argued that black studies courses should be taught by blacks and be open to blacks alone. Whites were squeezed out of some civil rights activities. It was argued that the exploitation that blacks had experienced in the United States over 300 years had made them so different from whites that there could be no coming together until the whole basis of the relationship had been changed. This was a reversal of the previous strategy of criticizing racial ideas and demanding that people be treated on their merits as individuals.

Black consciousness in South Africa will develop along lines different from those of the United States. Blacks within the present Republic of South Africa cannot but see themselves as Africans, as the indigenous people of a region in which whites are an immigrant minority. It is not the blacks who have to find a way of legitimating their presence or identity. In the struggle for liberation differences between ethnic groups (Zulu, Xhosa, Tswana, Venda, etc.) can be pushed into the background and ethnic consciousness can decline as racial consciousness increases. Once blacks have a proportionate share in political power ethnic differences may move into the foreground as they have done elsewhere.

This chapter has shown that while racial consciousness varies with social and political circumstances, there are discernible factors which underlie increases in its intensity. Any superordinate group will have its internal divisions. Each segment of that group or class within it will play a double game, seeking to use the P–B division to strengthen its bargaining position within the P group and using its position within that group to reinforce its privileges with respect to the members of the B group. The game is complicated by a whole series of factors outside the parties' control. Among them is the obvious consideration that, irrespective of race, some individuals are more talented or harder-working than others. Racial discrimination works to prevent the rise of competent members of the B group and the fall of incompetent members of the P group. Those who enjoy privilege may wish to keep members of the B group divided, but by drawing a racial boundary they stimulate them to develop a consciousness of oppression which helps them to mobilize a new strength and upset the prevailing equilibrium.

CHAPTER 6
Decreasing racial consciousness

Racial consciousness was defined in Chapter 1 as an awareness of physical features as socially significant. In Chapter 3 a contrast was drawn between societies, like those in Latin America, where physical features contribute to assessment of an individual's social position, and societies like those of the Deep South and South Africa, where physical features are used to assign an individual to membership in a group whose members share a distinctive social position. Racial consciousness is much higher in societies of the latter kind because the physical features are significant in a greater range of situations and the decisions that depend upon them are more important. The only way of eliminating racial consciousness is for people to be so mixed up that physical features are no longer socially significant. As Chapter 5 has shown, government policies can influence the speed at which this takes place, but since people usually do not want to be mixed up, the process is normally slow.

Circumstances in the United Kingdom offer an interesting comparison with those in Latin America and the United States, because the balance of individual and group influences is different. The non-white minorities are concentrated in the English cities, and for the most part in the run-down inner-city areas. They identify themselves in varying degrees by national origin, religion, and colour. Official statistics (see Table 6.1) list people from India as the largest group; many of these are Sikhs from the Punjab; others are Gujerati Hindus from western India, Gujerati Muslims from the same area, and Ismaili Muslims, most of whom (like a lot of the Sikhs and Gujeratis) were resident in East Africa prior to immigration into Britain. A large number of the Pakistani minority are Muslims from the Mirpur region, but there are also Christians from the cities. The

Table 6.1 Population born outside the United Kingdom, by year of entry and country of birth, Great Britain, Spring 1984 (thousands)

Country of birth	Year of entry					Total entrants	% White
	Pre 1955	1955-64	1965-74	1975-84	No reply		
Irish Republic	243	136	61	27	76	544	98
Old Commonwealth	32	15	27	46	5	125	98
New Commonwealth and Pakistan	147	379	509	288	77	1,400	21
East African Commonwealth	6	16	113	49	9	192	13
Rest of African Commonwealth	7	9	22	30	7	75	31
Caribbean Commonwealth	18	146	52	8	18	242	5
India	61	87	148	64	23	382	18
Bangladesh	0	5	10	20	2	38	0
Far East Commonwealth	10	23	44	38	3	118	36
Mediterranean Commonwealth	33	40	30	7	3	112	94
Remainder of New Commonwealth	8	12	19	9	4	51	36
Pakistan	5	41	72	63	9	189	2
Other European Community	92	70	62	78	23	326	98
Other Europe (excluding USSR)	105	37	47	25	14	229	96
Rest of the world (including USSR)	88	39	75	181	18	400	93
All outside UK*	769	746	863	718	213	3,310	57

* Includes 287,000 persons who gave a year of entry but did not state their country of birth.

(Source: Labour Force Survey, 1984)

third largest Asian minority is that of Chinese, mainly from Hong Kong. In numerical terms they are followed by the people from Bangladesh, who are Bengali-speaking Muslims and are mostly settled in London's East End. There is a significant black African minority, many of them Nigerians. The settlers listed as West Indian or Guyanese include people from the communities of Indian origin in Trinidad and Guyana as well as Afro-Caribbeans from Jamaica, Barbados, Dominica, Granada, Guyana, Montserrat, St Kitts, St Lucia, Trinidad, and other islands. To start with, they identified themselves by their country of origin but over the years they, like their children, have come increasingly to identify themselves as black. None of these groups is anywhere near as large as that of Afro-Americans who constitute over 10 per cent of the population of the United States. If all the non-white groups are added together they make just 6 per cent of the total population.

Table 6.1 is based upon replies given in the 1984 *Labour Force Survey*. Respondents were also asked how they would classify themselves. The results are set out in Table 6.2, showing the percentages of each group within five age categories. The Greek-speaking Cypriots, Turkish-speaking Cypriots, and Maltese who make up the 'Mediterranean Commonwealth' category in Table 6.1 are not included. Table 6.2 also reveals that a relatively large number of people describe themselves as being of mixed ethnic origin. From Table 6.3 it can be seen that about one in five non-white children were born to mothers who were born in the United Kingdom, most of whom will themselves have been non-white. Over 13 per cent of the children were classified as mixed by the parent interviewed in the survey and the proportion so classified is increasing. When read with the results of previous surveys these data confirm that the proportion of persons of mixed origin has been rising steadily. About 1 per cent of all couples are ethnically mixed, using the categories of Table 6.2, and the percentage would be much higher if, say, English–French or English–United States couples were counted as ethnically mixed. The *Labour Force Survey* found that there were about twice as many non-white husbands with white wives as there were white husbands with non-white wives; this is to be expected when the non-white men have immigrated earlier than the non-white women. Table 6.4 supports the observation that it is unusual for persons of West Indian origin and South Asian origin to marry (much more unusual than for persons of either group to marry whites). This is the more notable because many Guyanese and Trinidadians (who may have described themselves as West Indian in the *Survey*) are of Indian origin. A

Table 6.2 British population, by ethnic group and age, 1984

Percentages	Age					All persons
	Under 16	16–29	30–34	45–64 (men) 45–59 (women)	65 and over (men) 60 and over (women)	
White	21	21	20	20	18	100
West Indian or Guyanese	26	33	17	21	2	100
Indian	32	28	23	13	4	100
Pakistani	46	22	16	15	1	100
Bangladeshi	49	22	13	15	0	100
Chinese	29	31	26	12	2	100
African	28	36	21	13	2	100
Arab	16	41	34	9	0	100
Mixed	50	27	11	8	3	100
Other	31	23	31	12	4	100
Not stated	28	24	18	16	15	100
All ethnic groups	21	22	20	19	18	100

(Source: Labour Force Survey, 1984)

Table 6.3   Non-white children born in the United Kingdom, by age, ethnic group and mother's country of birth, Great Britain, Spring 1984 (thousands)

Child's ethnic group	Age of child			All children
	0-4	*5-9*	*10-14*	
West Indian or Guyanese				
UK-born mother	11	9	5	25
Overseas-born mother	23	24	40	87
Mother's birthplace not known	2	3	6	10
Indian				
UK-born mother	3	2	1	7
Overseas-born mother	75	65	50	189
Mother's birthplace not known	7	10	10	28
Pakistani or Bangladeshi				
UK-born mother	2	1	1	4
Overseas-born mother	58	34	37	129
Mother's birthplace not known	15	8	5	27
Mixed				
UK-born mother	27	16	10	52
Overseas-born mother	12	9	9	30
Mother's birthplace not known	2	1	2	5
Other non-white				
UK-born mother	5	2	1	8
Overseas-born mother	30	11	9	51
Mother's birthplace not known	2	0	0	3
All non-white				
UK-born mother	47	30	19	96
Overseas-born mother	198	144	145	486
Mother's birthplace not known	29	22	22	73

(*Source: Labour Force Survey*, 1984)

breakdown of the category 'other' might throw further light onto the processes of self-classification.

The difficulty of defining a category of persons of mixed origin brings out dramatically some of the main problems in the attempt to develop a social scientific study of racial relations, for it highlights the way in which popular ideas about who counts as mixed vary from one country to another and diverge from any scientific classification based upon genetic characters or the objective measurement of

Table 6.4 Couples: ethnic group of husband by ethnic group of wife, Great Britain, Spring 1984 (thousands)

Ethnic group of husband	Ethnic group of wife							All ethnic groups
	White	West Indian or Guyanese	Indian	Pakistani or Bangladeshi	Mixed	Other	Not stated	
White	12,819	11	4	1	11	15	39	12,900
West Indian or Guyanese	18	72	0	0	1	0	2	92
Indian	9	0	156	1	1	1	1	170
Pakistani or Bangladeshi	5	0	2	76	0	0	0	83
Mixed	10	0	0	1	10	1	0	22
Other	28	1	0	0	0	52	1	82
Not stated	10	0	0	0	0	0	149	160
All ethnic groups	12,899	85	162	79	22	70	192	13,509

(Source: Labour Force Survey, 1984)

variations in pigmentation. Nearly all the people who in Britain describe themselves as mixed would, in the United States, be accounted black unless they 'passed' for white. In most of Latin America they would not be distinguished as a group at all. In South Africa a section of the population numbering over 2.5 million (more than half the size of the white group) have traditionally been referred to as Coloured or Cape Coloured. Their history stretches back to the seventeenth century. The mass media outside South Africa have started calling them mixed race instead of Coloured (as if there was something wrong with that name). The expression 'mixed race' implies, unjustifiably, that there are pure races. To say that someone is of mixed race is to imply that his or her parents were of very different appearance, but in South Africa that person's parents, grandparents, and great-grandparents may have been of similar appearance to him or her. What counts as 'mixed' depends upon popular ideas and is often in conflict with any scientific assessment. A person who travelled from Britain to South Africa, to Latin America and to the United States could find that he or she was differently classified in these four regions.

When there is uncertainty about how a person is to be classified, much may depend upon how that person regards himself or herself. The boundaries between groups can change as a result of patterns of self-ascription. The substantial number of people in Britain who describe themselves as mixed reflects the relatively greater tolerance there of what are considered 'mixed marriages' than in South Africa or the United States. It reveals a greater fluidity in the definition of groups in Britain than in those other countries.

Group influences upon the definition of racial roles are strongest where groups occupy separate territory and when the rate of economic change is slow. It is easier to maintain an institutionalized pattern of racial discrimination in a rural area than in a city where the pressures to respond to people's non-racial roles are greater. In an industrial society alignments based upon class differences are enhanced, but differences of race may divide classes, while differences of class may divide social groups. Some minority leaders expect Afro-Caribbeans to become a more solidary group within the working-class political movement, but others see them as individualistic; attempts to create associations able to speak in their name have had only limited success. The South Asian groups are very diverse; their associations are those of the first generation of settlers still very much influenced by the culture they have brought with them.

POLICY

The circumstances which led to the Commonwealth Immigration Act of 1962 have been discussed in many books. It was a negative measure, an expedient resolution of a problem which had troubled governments caught between the pressures of domestic and Commonwealth politics. A better starting-point is the formulation of a positive policy for integration in 1965. This was summed up in the declaration that:

> no artificial barrier of race or colour should prevent any individual from developing his abilities to the full and from acquiring both the economic and social status to which his skills entitle him ... the major effort must be directed towards ensuring that the children of immigrants, who have either been born or received their education here, are treated on exactly the same terms as all other citizens and that their colour of skin becomes totally irrelevant. (See Cmnd. 4268:2.)

Among the consequences of this policy were legislation against racial discrimination, the empowering of the Home Secretary to make grants to those local authorities which had to make special provisions on account of immigration from the New Commonwealth (Local Government Act 1966, section 11) and the establishment of the Community Relations Commission to assist and co-ordinate the many community relations councils being set up with local authority support throughout the country. The policy of integration can be seen as designed to reduce racial consciousness in favour of an awareness of shared citizenship.

If the policy was to succeed it had first to bring about major changes in white attitudes. The whites regarded a dark complexion as a sign that a person belonged elsewhere, probably in India or one of the colonies. Surveys in 1951 and 1956 recorded respectively 38 per cent and 18 per cent of the population of England and Wales as being opposed to free entry to Britain for immigrant workers from the colonies (Banton 1983b). It was assumed that they were temporary visitors who would return to their own countries and that it was to Britain's advantage to permit entry as part of a constitutional arrangement which brought economic benefits to the 'mother country'. It was part of this pattern that when asked about how to provide housing for these workers 79 per cent and 81 per cent of respondents in these surveys considered that the best course was to 'provide hostels for them'. At this time there was no conception of New Commonwealth settlers buying their own houses, or qualifying for council housing. Only rarely were they seen as competing with white people for houses, jobs, and other services. The sense of 'us' and 'them' was very much stronger in the 1950s. To start with, many English people were unaware that the mother tongue of black West Indians was English. Many knew hardly anything about differences between the immigrant groups. The author remembers a Nigerian telling him in 1951 how his employer had called him to explain to two Bengali-speakers the nature of the work for which they had been engaged, as if, because they both had dark complexions, a Nigerian and a Bangladeshi would understand one another's speech.

As immigration from the West Indies and the Indian subcontinent increased in the late 1950s, white consciousness of competition grew. Opposition to free entry for New Commonwealth immigrants rose rapidly. The public thought there was an immigration problem. The stopping, or reversing, of immigration was the best way to deal with any problem of racial relations. The years from 1965 to 1968 were a period in which the government tried, with some success, to reorient white opinion and to help whites see that such assumptions were unrealistic. Nevertheless, they and successive governments have been criticized for failing to confront white racism. Their policies have been disparaged as 'too little and too late'. It is said that instead of racial relations getting better they have got worse, and some of the evidence can indeed support such a pessimistic conclusion. For example, the incidence of racial attacks (mostly cases of young white males attacking Asians in the streets and, on occasion, of setting fire to their homes) became a cause for concern in the late 1970s and 1980s; there are no figures permitting a proper comparison with the 1950s and 1960s, but the incidence of racial attacks surely increased over this period. In 1986 the House of Commons Home Affairs Committee described them as 'the most shameful and dispiriting aspect of race relations in Britain'. To appreciate why some things should appear to have got worse while others were getting better it is necessary to understand the shifts in the expectations of both minority and majority members, and the effects of change in the total society.

The government itself soon appreciated that the provisions of the 1965 Race Relations Act were insufficient. Many commentators had maintained all along that an Act which penalized discrimination only in places of public resort like dance-halls, restaurants, and hotels would fail to deal with the source of the trouble; but persuading the public, and Parliament, of this took longer. It was often said that laws could not change attitudes and that only education could remove prejudice. Racial discrimination (the unfavourable treatment of persons on racial grounds) was often confounded with racial

97

prejudice (an emotional and rigidly unfavourable attitude towards persons assigned to a racial group). The relations between the two are now better understood. Discrimination is often caused by prejudice, but sometimes unprejudiced people discriminate; for example, when they are ordered to do so. Prejudice often leads to discrimination but prejudiced people do not discriminate if they are afraid that they may be punished for doing so. When racial discrimination is customary and expected, this tends to encourage prejudice, so that laws against discrimination can have an educational value.

A particularly important contribution to the campaign for better legislation was made by an investigation carried out by Political and Economic Planning (PEP) (now the Policy Studies Institute (PSI)) in 1966-67. Three testers were employed, an Englishman, a Hungarian, and a West Indian. They were of similar age and good appearance. Claiming identical qualifications, they applied for jobs, for housing, for car insurance, and certain other services. When they sought jobs, the Englishman got 15 offers out of 40 firms; the Hungarian applying to the same firms for the same jobs got 10, and the West Indian 1. Out of 60 applications to rent accommodation, in 15 cases all three were treated alike. On 38 occasions the Englishman and the Hungarian were told the accommodation was available and the West Indian turned away. On 4 occasions the West Indian was asked for a higher rent; on 1 occasion both the West Indian and the Hungarian were asked for a higher rent. On 2 occasions the Englishman was the only person to be told that the accommodation was available to him. Asking for a higher rent is an example of a colour tax: this is the price differential paid by persons of a different colour to obtain services of a quality similar to those obtained by persons not subject to discrimination. Such a tax was also evident in respect of car insurance. All three testers claimed identical driving records. In 6 out of 20 applications the West Indian was refused insurance cover altogether; on 11 occasions he was quoted a higher premium. The average premiums quoted by the 14 firms who offered cover to all three testers were: West Indian £58, Hungarian £49, Englishman £45. In this, as in other parts of the study, the experience of the testers proved that the incidence of discrimination was higher than minority people had themselves estimated in interviews. The findings of the 1966-67 studies attracted much shocked comment in the press and helped create a climate of opinion in which the Home Secretary could persuade Parliament to extend the 1965 Race Relations Act to cover discrimination in employment, housing, and financial services.

Several other studies have measured discrimination by responding to advertisements. Two similar applications have been submitted for each job, one in the name of a white British applicant and the other from someone with a foreign-sounding name, or someone giving his birthplace as being in another country. When both applicants have been invited to an interview this has been treated as a case of 'no discrimination', but when one has been invited and not the other this has been recorded as evidence of discrimination. Such a measure probably underestimates the actual level of discrimination since some applicants invited for interview may be rejected at that stage on racial grounds. Tests conducted by the Policy Studies Institute in 1984–85 when compared with the results of similar tests conducted in 1973–74 show no significant change over the period. During those eleven years unemployment increased from less than 3 to over 13 per cent so it might not have been surprising had the incidence of discrimination increased. In the 1984–85 tests 335 vacancies in selected occupations were singled out and applications submitted in the names of three people otherwise similar except that one was of English, one Asian, and one West Indian origin. In 46 per cent of cases all three applicants received positive replies. In 25 per cent the English applicant was the only one to receive a positive reply. The results may be summarized as in Table 6.5. At least one-third of employers were discriminating against either Asians or West Indians, and at least one employer in five was discriminating against both (Brown and Gay 1985).

Table 6.5 Applicants called for interview, 1984–85

Outcomes	Total	English	Asian	West Indian
% Positive	72	90	63	63
% Negative	28	10	37	37
Total	1,005	335	335	335

(*Source:* Brown and Gay 1985)

Other research suggests that while there is much more discrimination against people with dark skins, the black–white split is not as sharp as in the United States. A study of applications by post for jobs in accountancy and financial management showed that the chances of being called for interview varied with nationality. Applications from ostensibly British persons had an 85 per cent success rate. Otherwise similar applications from ostensibly Australian persons, a 75 per cent rate; the rates for the French were 68, for Africans 53, West Indians 48, Indians and Pakistanis 44 per cent. There is a continuous scale of degrees of distance in which a dark complexion is a powerfully negative factor. The assignment of racial status in Britain does not follow the colour-caste model. It is a continuous scale of differentiation which in some circumstances shows a steep slope.

LAW AND ITS ENFORCEMENT

One of the most important ways of reducing racial discrimination is to declare it unlawful, imposing sanctions upon discriminators and providing remedies to victims. It then becomes necessary to determine the scope of the law. For example, in 1985 two women in North Wales were refused employment as care assistants in old people's homes because they could not speak Welsh. They applied to an industrial tribunal which judged that they had been discriminated against on the ground of their race. Gwynedd County Council took the case to an employment appeal tribunal which ruled that while language might be one indicator of membership in a racial group it was wrong in law to use this factor as a criterion in isolation. The appeal tribunal was disinclined to accept that someone from Holyhead who spoke Welsh was of a different racial group from someone who spoke English. So they allowed the appeal.

The leading case in this field is that of *Mandla* v. *Dowell Lee*. It arose from the action of the headmaster of a private school in Birmingham. This was a multiracial but Christian school. Among the 305 pupils were 5 Sikhs, 34 Hindus, 6 blacks and 7 Chinese. The Sikh pupils did not wear turbans. Mr Mandla wanted his son to attend, and to wear his turban. The headmaster was willing to admit the boy provided he did not wear a turban, because the headmaster's policy was to emphasize what the boys had in common and to minimize differences. Ironically, the father would not have wished his son to attend this school had he understood that all boys had to attend classes in the Christian faith. When he learned of the headmaster's decision, he persuaded the Commission for Racial Equality to bring a case in the County Court. The judge there ruled that Sikhs were not a racial group within the meaning of the 1976 Act. The evidence called in the case indicated rather that the Sikhs were a religious group and discrimination on grounds of religion is not contrary to law. The Commission for Racial Equality appealed. The Court of Appeal had to decide whether discrimination directed against turban-wearing was discrimination on the grounds of colour, race, nationality, or ethnic or national origins. All three judges declared that it was not covered by the adjective 'ethnic' because ethnic meant 'pertaining to race'. The Commission for Racial

Equality then persuaded the House of Lords to consider a further appeal where five Law Lords took note of a New Zealand decision that Jews in that country formed a group with common ethnic origins. They declared that to be an ethnic group in law, a group had to regard itself, and be regarded by others, as distinct by virtue of a shared history and cultural tradition. Characteristics of geography, language, literature, religion, and minority status might be relevant though not essential. Therefore they found that Sikhs were covered by section 3 of the Act and that the headmaster had been wrong.

The House of Lords found that the 'no-turban' rule constituted indirect discrimination. It would have been direct discrimination if the boy had been turned away because he was a Sikh. That had not happened; after all, there were already five Sikhs attending the school. He was turned away because the headmaster applied a condition concerning school uniform with which it was more difficult for Sikhs to comply, and he had not shown this condition to be necessary to the school. Indirect discrimination occurs when someone imposes on another a condition which:

(a) is such that the proportion of persons of the same racial group as that other who can comply with it is considerably smaller than the proportion of persons not of that racial group who can comply with it;
(b) he cannot show to be justifiable irrespective of the colour, race, nationality, or ethnic or national origin of the person to whom it is applied;
(c) is to the detriment of that other because he cannot comply with it.

The distinction between direct and indirect discrimination covers that which social scientists draw between categorical and statistical discrimination. The social science distinction turns upon the motivation of the discriminator. Categorical discrimination is discrimination against all members of a category because they are socially assigned to that category. So no blacks or no Jews or no women are admitted to some club. Statistical discrimination is discrimination against persons assigned to a category because of a belief that those in that category are less likely to have attributes that are being sought. Thus an employer faced with a very large number of applications for a post might eliminate from consideration all applications from blacks, Jews, or women if this was a kind of work in which blacks, Jews, or women had not previously been employed and therefore he thought them less likely to have the required skills. He might agree that some blacks, Jews, or women might have these skills, but believe it improbable so that it would be a waste of his time to investigate the qualifications of such applicants when he had so many other applicants who seemed suitable.

In law there is no concept of positive discrimination. In 1985 a group called the Women's Reproduction Information Centre in London advertised for a part-time advice worker. A white applicant from the United States was told by letter that it had been decided 'to short-list women of ethnic origin only' (note how a minus-one conception of ethnicity was extended to include white Americans!). The woman alleged before an industrial tribunal that this was in breach of the Race Relations Act. The centre admitted that it had no defence and was ordered to pay £250 compensation. Similarly, three white men claimed that on account of their race or colour they had been refused jobs as gardening apprentices by Hackney Borough Council. In 1986 a court declared that though the council might be seeking to redress what it considered to be the effect of past discrimination, this did not justify the discrimination against the three men.

The nearest approach in the 1976 Act to positive discrimination occurs in sections 35, 37, and 38, which make it lawful to afford training and comparable services to members of particular racial groups to enable them to compete on an equal basis with others for employment. Thus the police in the West Midlands, in their attempt to increase the number of black and Asian police officers, have mounted courses to help selected candidates, primarily blacks, who failed the entrance examination the first time. They have to reach the same standard as other recruits, but they are helped to reach it. Such programmes are now described as positive action.

How can it be proved that someone discriminated on racial grounds? There are two main ways. The first can be used when the person in question has said something which suggested that his or her action was racially motivated. The second can be used when examination of one individual's behaviour towards people of different race reveals a discriminatory pattern. Some of the cases that have been successfully brought have used both methods. The *Annual Report of the Commission for Racial Equality* for 1986 provides a sample. Thus in Tyne and Wear a taxi-driver of Pakistani origin, Mr Khan, applied for a vacant job. Speaking over the telephone, with a local 'Geordie' accent, he volunteered the information that he was of Asian origin. The proprietress of the company then said, 'Oh, I'm really sorry but I cannot afford to employ coloured people because it affects my business. ... My customers won't take lightly to coloured drivers. .... I'm not prejudiced, it's the business.' Mr Khan later discovered that just afterwards two white drivers were engaged. When brought before an industrial tribunal the company admitted that it had acted unlawfully, undertook not to discriminate again, and paid Mr Khan £750 compensation. A comparable case from London concerned Mrs Motala, a conveyancing clerk of Indian origin. When she telephoned about a job in a solicitor's office she was told that the position had been filled. So Mrs Motala's friend also telephoned. The employer asked if she was English. He said he wanted someone who spoke 'proper English'. Later she too was told that the position had been filled. Mrs Motala then got an Australian friend to telephone. She was told that the job was available. From this evidence an industrial tribunal concluded that there had been direct discrimination and awarded £300 compensation.

The distinction between direct and indirect discrimination is recalled in two cases of pressure to discriminate. In one, a firm of chartered accountants admitted that, when giving details of a vacancy to Leeds Careers Service, one of its employees had said 'As the office is rather racialist, could we have a white girl?' The industrial tribunal recorded a contravention; the company undertook to avoid any repetition; it agreed to adopt an equal opportunity policy based upon the commission's Code of Practice and to notify all job vacancies to the relevant job centres or careers offices. In the other case the managing director of a Liverpool printing company refused to consider a Chinese woman for a secretary/assistant manager position, saying he wanted only people with an English accent. The tribunal found that the imposition of this requirement constituted indirect discrimination. It recorded the director's undertaking to notify all vacancies to job centres or careers service offices, to introduce a monitored equal opportunities policy, and to inform the commission of its operation.

The Race Relations Act empowers the Commission for Racial Equality to issue codes of practice to promote equal opportunity. It gives the commission important powers to undertake formal investigations in connection with their duty to work for the elimination of racial discrimination. If, as a result of an investigation, it concludes that discrimination is occurring, it may issue a notice requiring a person or a company to make changes. If this does not bring about the desired result the commission can then bring proceedings in the civil courts. The criminal courts will deal with any charge of incitement to racial hatred. This is now defined as the publication (in speech or writing) of words threatening, abusive, or insulting to members of a racial group with either the intention or the likely effect of stirring up hatred against them.

The law relating to racial relations focuses on a discontinuity. An action or practice is either discriminatory or not discriminatory. A statement either constitutes incitement or it does not. Social science, by contrast, deals with continuities. Given that a black house-purchaser may have to pay more to buy a house, or a black worker may be paid a lower wage, it is necessary to explain why the house-purchaser has to pay that much more and why the employee is paid that much less. That is not the lawyer's concern but the social scientist's. A variety of factors are involved in determining the level of discrimination. Some derive from the attitudes and objectives of the discriminator, others from the structure of the market within which it occurs, but one in particular deserves mention, and that is the form of competition. Where racially distinctive people compete with one another as groups, discrimination is likely to take the form of exclusion. In the Deep South, whites tried to reserve certain occupations for themselves and allowed others to be Negro jobs. There were similar, but less successful, attempts in Northern industries. White workers would make life difficult for black co-workers and try to force them out. The best opportunities for black workers arose when the whites went on strike and employers were ready to engage blacks to replace them, but this, of course, increased the hostility of white workers. Black workers could get jobs only in such circumstances or by being willing to work for lower wages. Once they had secured a position in an industry then the white unions were under pressure to admit them to union membership because only by representing the great majority of workers could the unions hope to exercise much bargaining power. Therefore blacks had to pay a kind of colour tax to get into a wide range of occupations, but once they were in, the level of wage discrimination would have declined because of pressure from white as well as black workers. The cost-conscious employer does not wish to pay anyone more than he has to. The more competitive the market, the more he is pushed to judge workers on their economic qualities. Unless other factors intervene, this will bring down the level of discrimination, so the structure of markets is very important to the maintenance or reduction of inequalities of opportunity.

DISCRIMINATION AND DISADVANTAGE

The 1976 Act established the Commission for Racial Equality and charged it to 'work towards the elimination of discrimination' and 'to promote . . . good relations between persons of different racial groups generally'. It did not seek to define racial equality, which would be difficult in view of the many ways in which this expression can be used. It may clarify matters if a distinction is drawn between equality (or inequality) as a moral judgement in political life and equality (or inequality) as a matter of measurement for the purposes of social science. The number 5 is not equal to the number 6. In the army, the pay of a private is not equal to that of a major. Differentials in rewards may be necessary to attract people to undertake dangerous jobs or to provide an incentive to promotion in a hierarchical organization. How people feel about inequalities is another matter altogether. Some of them are regarded as just, others as excessive. The amount an individual earns is often regarded as a private matter, so others may not know enough about inequalities of income or the reasons for them that they should have any feelings about whether or not they are justified. This relates back to the questions discussed earlier about the circumstances in which individuals become conscious of belonging to groups. It also relates to changes in the extent of inequality. Groups which mobilize to press the claims of their members and to exert pressure may be able to change their relative position and increase or decrease inequalities.

While discrimination is a very important source of such inequalities, there are other sources which are less easily attacked by legal measures. For example, people who do not understand the majority language will be handicapped in the employment market. It has been established that, in the white group, the children of relatively uneducated parents are at a disadvantage in school by comparison with the children of parents who can do more in the home to help their children's educational progress. If there are such differences within the majority, they may also be found between the majority and some of the minorities. This was officially recognized in 1980–81 when the Subcommittee on Race Relations and Immigration of the House of Commons Home Affairs Committee published a report entitled *Racial Disadvantage*. For studying the causes of racial inequality, racial disadvantage is the basic concept because it covers a wider field than that of racial discrimination. Racial disadvantage is any form of handicap associated with assignment to a racial group. It is exemplified by the Gypsies. Children brought up in a group that travels around in mobile homes undertaking casual and seasonal work are likely to be at a disadvantage when it comes to educational attainment and all the jobs that depend upon educational qualifications. That disadvantage can be seen as stemming primarily from the unconscious decision of the group to live as they do. The same can be said of religious groups in the United States, like the Amish, who live as separate farming communities. They do not permit their children to go to ordinary schools lest they there learn ideas that will dissuade them from following a way of life which the parental and grandparental generation believe to be in accordance with the Bible's commands.

Research shows that racial disadvantage varies in a continuous fashion as between groups of different kinds, and over time. The speed at which immigrant disadvantage is reduced depends in part upon motivation. Refugees may be anxious to return to their country of origin. They may not utilize all the opportunities open to them in the new country and so, instead of catching up with the majority population, they may remain behind them in their economic attainments. Other immigrants are distinguished by their high work motivation; they have come to a new land to make their fortunes; they work harder than the native workers and catch up or surpass them in their earnings. Barry R. Chiswick (1979) concluded from a study of six immigrant groups in the United States, and from research relating to three other countries, that male economic immigrants catch up with the native-born workers who have similar economic characteristics by the time they have been in the country eleven to sixteen years; thereafter their earnings are higher. Their sons also have earnings 5–10 per cent higher. Among refugees, because their skills are less transferable and their motivations different, earnings are lower and may never catch up. Some groups are more successful than others either because of higher motivation or more entrepreneurial skill. Some groups are held back by racial discrimination, even if some individuals work all the harder to prove that they are as industrious as anyone else.

In Britain in the mid 1970s it looked as if Afro-Caribbean and South Asian groups, despite racial discrimination, might be catching up at a rate comparable to the groups studied by Chiswick because many of the West Indians would have emigrated just before the 1962 Immigration Act came into force (see Table 6.2 for the age structure of these minorities). Two surveys in 1974 and 1975 showed that non-white workers, both male and female, were earning more than white workers in the bottom two out of six occupational categories. This was doubtless due in some measure to their being on average younger, more ready to work extra hours, and work in shifts. While native workers often have set expectations about the kinds of employment they should undertake, economic migrants are more flexible and, if unemployed, more likely to take different sorts of job, perhaps jobs which many native workers would consider beneath their dignity. The findings of more recent studies suggest, however, that the economic progress of New Commonwealth immigrants is being retarded by white discrimination, but the comparisons are far from simple.

The commonest way of comparing relative disadvantage is by comparing group distributions or averages at two points in time. For example, the percentage of non-whites in the six classes of the Registrar-General's scale in the 1981 census relative to whites might be set against the figures for 1971 to see how much change there had been; or the average earnings of non-whites recorded in the *General Household Survey* on two dates could be compared with the average earnings of whites. One problem to watch out for is that the population of New Commonwealth origin changed significantly between 1971 and 1981. A new generation of young people entered the labour market and they formed a higher proportion of the minority population. There were also important differences within that population. The 1982 PSI survey found that Indians from India had the highest earnings, followed by Asians from Africa, then West Indians, Pakistanis, and last of all Bangladeshis (Brown 1984: 180, 216). There is reason to believe that the Indians from India were the best educated, most able to speak English, and had the most marketable skills. They had been in this country longer than the Bangladeshis, who were least educated. Of the main groups, West Indians emigrated first, followed by Indians, Pakistanis, and Bangladeshis, so proportionately more of the 1970s immigration was from Bangladesh and this will have depressed the rate at which the New Commonwealth group as a whole was catching up during the 1970s.

In comparing the economic progress of groups it is important to allow for changes in the overall level of unemployment. In 1974 (a time of relatively full employment), unemployment rates among non-whites were about the same as among whites. By 1982, when the general level of employment had fallen, unemployment was higher among all ethnic minority groups than among whites. The decline in the textiles industry had a particularly severe effect upon unemployment among Bangladeshi women. Immigrant groups are often over-represented in particular kinds of employment so it may come to seem natural, for example, that Jews or Asians go in for sewing garments and Chinese for the restaurant trade. This is not because they have any special aptitude for such trades or have practised them before migration. Immigrants seek out the best opportunities and often secure particular niches in the economic structure as a result. If these trades are hit by depression more than other trades, then minority workers suffer more. It is also important to note that when vacancies outnumber job-seekers, the tendency of some employers to discriminate racially will not prevent the determined minority worker from obtaining employment. But when vacancies are few, employer discrimination will have a greater influence on minority unemployment levels. When the general level of employment falls it is the less skilled jobs which are hit hardest, and, within these as within other job categories, it is the minority workers who are likely to be declared redundant first.

Catch-up rates can be based upon kinds of employment or upon earnings. A comparison of surveys in 1974 and 1982 shows that the percentage of Afro-Caribbean men in professional and managerial jobs increased over this period from 2 to 7 per cent; the proportion of Asian men in such jobs increased from 7 to 14 per cent; the proportion of whites fell slightly from 23 to 22 per cent (see Field 1986). Asian females did rather better. In semi-skilled and unskilled work there was little indication of any closing of the gap. The percentage of Afro-Caribbean men in such jobs rose from 32 to 34, whereas the corresponding percentages of whites and Asians both fell. The proportions of women of all groups in such jobs fell. In 1982 the gross earnings of male minority full-time employees averaged £110–£120 per week against £129 for white employees, while in no job level did male minority earnings match those of whites. Even allowing for the possibility of a greater unwillingness on the part of the minority men with the higher incomes to say how much they actually earned, it looks as if there was no diminution of the white–non-white earnings differential over the previous eight years (Brown 1984: 180, 214, 330). The economic restructuring which took place since 1974 benefited those employed in the sunrise industries and hit those employed in the smokestack industries. It increased the gap between rich and poor in both the majority and the minority groups. It looks as if during the last decade the number of minority people in middle-class positions quadrupled and that about 10 per cent of male minority workers are now in professional and managerial jobs.

ATTITUDES

Though there has been a black presence in Britain for more than four centuries, the present phase started with the arrival in 1948 of the SS

Empire Windrush bringing 492 Jamaican settlers (491 of them men). In the four decades since then attitudes have changed in many ways. White hostility to immigration increased sharply at the end of the 1950s and has remained at a high level. At the same time white acceptance of non-whites as fellow workers, neighbours, and fellow citizens has increased. The first generation of immigrants was comprised of men and women who were relatively ambitious and adaptable. They came in search of opportunity and put up with many hardships. Their children had higher expectations of the English. Parents were often angered more by the disadvantages suffered by their children than by those which they themselves had experienced. Since the late 1960s, white people have been made to confront evidence that not only were whites discriminating consciously but that some of the practices they took for granted were unintentionally discriminatory. For example, when they have a job vacancy many employers have been accustomed to offer this position to someone recommended by one of their existing employees. They see this as making for a happier and more co-operative workforce. Yet if all their employees are white, non-whites never get an opportunity of employment in such a firm.

The Coventry plant of Massey-Ferguson, the tractor manufacturers, provided a related example. In 1979, out of about 5,000 workers, there were just three Afro-Caribbeans and three Asians, although a much higher proportion of blacks and Asians in the locality would have been qualified to fill vacancies at the plant. When the Commission for Racial Equality investigated the circumstances it found that the main reason for this under-representation was the company's method of recruitment for hourly paid jobs. It did not advertise or notify vacancies to job centres, but gave preference to those who submitted letters of application written in good English. When jobs were becoming vacant the existing workers naturally tended to pass on the news to other whites, as friends, relatives, or neighbours. One case of direct discrimination was uncovered, but the most important finding was that the company's methods of recruitment entailed discriminatory practices with respect to hourly paid employees and acted as barriers to equality of opportunity with respect to apprentices and youth trainees. The company co-operated fully with the investigation and, on its conclusion, agreed to work with the Commission to maintain a comprehensive, effective, and well-monitored equal opportunities programme. It often requires an intervention of this sort to capitalize upon positive attitudes and bring about changes.

Prejudiced whites have described blacks as work-shy and unwilling to accept authority; they have said that both blacks and Asians are unwilling to integrate into British society. To such stereotypes others have counterposed an image of blacks as the victims of white racism, alienated from British society. In so doing they have played down differences between and within the racial minorities and have failed to overcome the implication that blacks have been so damaged by white prejudice that they are people to whom things happen rather than people able to act for themselves. The findings of social research are quite contrary to both of these images. They show that ethnic minority people in general, and young blacks in particular, are no more hostile to established institutions than are those who correspond to them in age and social status in the white population. When blacks are critical they criticize particular practices, like those they see as police harassment, and failures to implement policies properly, rather than white society generally. As has already been pointed out, Hindus and Muslims often condemn what they see as the sexual immorality of whites and their failure to look after properly orphans and elderly relatives. Significant numbers of all ethnic minorities say that they themselves have not experienced discrimination, or that they believe it to be exceptional. If anything, black and Asian pupils have more positive attitudes towards school than do whites. Studies suggest that young black and Asian people are just as likely as young whites to register as unemployed, use career advisers, job centres, and other services (Field 1984). In forming their views about British society, ethnic minority members usually compare it with that of their country of origin, and then usually in Britain's favour. If these reasons come as a surprise, the reader should reflect upon the power of popular consciousness to distort the truth.

Gallup poll data show that the expression of social distance towards coloured people declined substantially over the period 1964–81 (Table 6.6). The total saying that they would accept coloured people as neighbours went up from 49 to 59 per cent; as friends from 45 to 78 per cent; as schoolfellows to their children from 54 to 78 per cent; as fellow workers from 61 to 82 per cent; as a principal or employer from 35 to 63 per cent; as son-in-law from 15 to 35 per cent; as daughter-in-law from 16 to 37 per cent. These reductions measure the extent to which white behaviour was deracialized in that appearance was no longer taken to be a sign indicating that the other person was unacceptable as party to a relationship. But it is important to notice that the social distance expressed towards immigrants was declining at the same time as hostility towards further immigration was increasing. If someone expressed hostility

Table 6.6 Changes in social distance expressed by whites

Which of these four phrases best describes how you would feel about having coloured people....

	November 1964				May 1981			
	Pleased	Not mind	Rather not	Strongly dislike	Pleased	Not mind	Rather not	Strongly dislike
(a) as neighbours?	5	44	26	17	2	57	28	10
(b) as friends?	5	40	21	12	10	68	13	5
(c) as schoolfellows to your children?	4	50	16	11	6	72	11	4
(d) as fellow workers?	4	57	16	13	6	76	10	4
(e) as your principal or employer?	2	33	22	28	3	60	16	13
(f) as your son-in-law?	2	13	27	44	3	32	25	33
(g) as your daughter-in-law?	2	14	26	44	3	34	24	33

(*Source:* Gallup poll)

111

towards immigration that did not necessarily mean that he or she felt hostile towards immigrants already settled in Britain. Measures of social distance make possible the study of this social dimension to the expression of prejudice and pinpoint the sorts of situations in which discrimination is most likely.

Table 6.6 might suggest that racial relations in Britain have been 'getting better'. Against such an inference must be set the contrary findings from opinion polls. Surveys conducted for the Commission for Racial Equality in 1975 and 1981 found that the proportion of whites believing that relations were getting worse increased by 65 per cent, whereas among both West Indians and Asians three times as many thought they were getting worse in 1981 than had given this reply six years earlier (Anwar 1986: 27). The urban rioting in Bristol in 1980 and in Brixton and other places in the Summer of 1981 may have strengthened the impression of deterioration since young blacks played a prominent part in nearly all these riots. That impression must have been strong before the main sequence of rioting because the interviewing for the 1981 survey was completed by 23rd March. In the 1982 PSI survey most white respondents testified that white people had come to accept people of West Indian and Asian origin, while at the same time agreeing that white people did not understand the way of life of people in these groups. West Indians and Asians also thought that whites had accepted them but insisted more strongly that their way of life was not understood. Asked whether there was more discrimination than five years earlier, 39 per cent of whites, 43 per cent of West Indians, and 45 per cent of Asians said there was more (the percentages replying that there was less were 33, 21, and 7 per cent respectively). In both 1974 and 1982 the PSI asked respondents: 'In general, do you think life in Britain is now better for people of Asian/West Indian origin than it was five years ago, is it worse or has there been no change?' The proportion of West Indians and Asians saying that life had got worse for them rose from 16 to 18 per cent respectively in 1974 to 53 and 51 per cent eight years later. Those saying that life had got better fell from 54 and 35 per cent in 1974 to 20 and 15 per cent in 1982 (Brown 1984: 277–86). The main reasons given for the reported deterioration were economic: recession, unemployment, and inflation. There was no blanket condemnation of white people or white institutions as racially biased. When asked about discrimination, blacks and whites gave varying responses in respect of the police, courts, schools, trade unions, insurance companies, and pubs, showing that they evaluated relations in different settings independently.

Members of the ethnic minorities now demand equal treatment more confidently than they did in the 1960s. Whites are better informed about the nature and incidence of discrimination. In expressing a belief that racial prejudice is increasing, white respondents may, however, be reflecting messages from the mass media, rather than reporting on something of which they have personal knowledge. Those who are responsible for the preparation of TV programmes and those who write for the newspapers may see white prejudice as a problem which, if unchecked, is likely to cause increasing social conflict and economic cost in the future. If so, they may try to persuade their audiences of the seriousness of the situation: to do so they may highlight instances of conflict, prejudice, and discrimination; thereby they will build an image of relations as being worse than might appear from a statistical measure of their frequency. This would help explain why so many people believe that relations have got worse. If at the same time white people's own sentiments have become more positive it would not be surprising if they concluded that the decline must have been caused by an increase in prejudice among other people. When matters are so complex it is difficult to come to any general conclusion other than that relations may have been getting 'better' on some measures and 'worse' on others.

One way of reducing prejudice is to bring individuals to acknowledge that they have been using ideas about people's race as signs of expected behaviour. They can be asked to justify this, though such an approach can be counter-productive if it puts the person on the defensive. To get a man to see that he has been using a wrong minus sign in his arithmetic is easier than to get him to acknowledge that he has been using a wrong minus sign in deciding how to treat others. This is in part because of the many-strandedness of social relations and the way that almost everything someone does has sign value in indicating the sort of person he or she is, or wishes to be thought. Anything which indicates that someone may not share informal understandings points to a possible risk and many people are anxious to avoid risks. It may be possible to persuade a man that he has been using a wrong criterion if there is evidence that he has exaggerated the risk. In general, though, it may be better to try to secure agreement with him as to what are the right criteria, particularly those of fairness. To stress positive standards and ways of attaining them can be a way of reducing the sensitivity that people display when they are criticized. Those who emphasize the depth of white prejudice and the frequency of discrimination build up an

113

image of an insoluble problem and encourage defeatism. If people believe that the problem can be overcome they are more likely to contribute to efforts designed to this end.

The British electoral system makes it more difficult for racial minorities to achieve equal representation in the House of Commons (though it is within the power of the government to see that they are represented in the House of Lords). The electoral system requires that the candidate who achieves most votes represent all the residents in a territorial constituency. To succeed, a candidate has first to be chosen as the official candidate of a major party. In a 'safe seat' this ensures almost automatic election to the House of Commons. Elsewhere the strength of the parties may be evenly balanced and if one candidate makes himself or herself unpopular or is someone with whom electors cannot easily identify themselves, the vote may swing to the other side. If therefore an ethnic minority comprises less than a third of the residents the parties may be reluctant to choose a candidate from that minority less it lose them the votes of majority people. However, once a kind of psychological 'tipping point' has been passed and a minority person elected who is seen as representing all the constituents, then the British electoral system works to reduce racial consciousness. If racial characters are no longer a major factor determining whether someone is a potential candidate, minority people may be selected to a degree more than proportionate to their numbers in the population. In Britain there has for a long time been a higher proportion of Jews as Members of Parliament than in the country and they have achieved prominence in all the major parties. This has greatly favoured the integration of that minority into the life of the nation.

The general election of 1987 resulted in the return to the House of Commons of twenty-three Jewish MPs. They constituted 3.6 per cent of the House, whereas Jews are a little over 0.6 per cent of the total population. The election resulted in the return of three black MPs representing London constituencies and one Asian MP from Leicester. Together they constituted 0.6 per cent of the House of Commons, whereas blacks and Asians were 3.6 per cent of the total population. In the 1960s nearly all Jewish MPs represented the Labour Party but by 1987 twice as many as those in the Labour Party sat on the Conservative side. The black and Asian MPs are all Labour. Studies show that both Afro-Caribbean and Asian voters are more inclined to support the Labour Party, even after making allowance for differences of socio-economic status (Anwar 1986: 74,78), but these MPs could not have been elected without the support of whites voting on party rather than racial lines.

Those who left New Commonwealth countries to settle in Britain came with the hope that they would make their way in the new country as individuals or as members of family groups. They did not see themselves as members of racial or ethnic minorities. Only in Britain did they acquire a consciousness of themselves as members of minorities. They turned first to fellow countrymen for mutual aid and friendship. Then they developed a fellow-feeling with others whom they saw as sharing their struggles. In the mid 1960s, influenced by events in the United States, some of the politically engaged Afro-Caribbeans started to refer to their group as black instead of coloured. Then a few years later they started to use it as a synonym for non-white, counting as black everyone who was liable to be an object of white racial prejudice. Some of the younger South Asians, particularly those born in Britain, began to accept this as a designation for themselves.

This tendency has been the stronger because, as has been seen, there is in Britain no agreement upon any single name or set of names appropriate for designating those who in official statistics are identified as NCWP, that is, people whose origins lie primarily in the New Commonwealth with Pakistan. By the mid 1980s it appeared as if very many, perhaps most, white people in ordinary conversation would use the adjective 'coloured', whereas most Labour Party activists, most social scientists, most white people working in the mass media, and most Afro-Caribbeans would make a point of saying 'black'. Young people might be more inclined than their elders to favour the new usage. The use of the name black in a sense synonymous with non-white had been increased by the policies of the Greater London Council, the struggle over black sections in the Labour Party, the advertising of posts for 'black social workers' and the like, in which black has been given this inclusive connotation. Whereas in the 1950s 'black' was usually felt to be insulting and 'coloured' acceptable, now it is often the other way round.

THE BATTLE OF THE NAME

The pressure to use black as a synonym for non-white should be seen as a political struggle. Groups adopt new names for themselves in order to express a feeling that the nature of their group is no longer adequately represented by the previously prevailing name. They adopt new names for other groups either to satisfy members of those groups who want a change, or to indicate that the relationship has changed. Afro-Americans rejected coloured in favour of black. In South Africa the adjective 'Native' has been discarded; 'black' is widely used because it is preferred by black Africans; probably the government would sooner not call them Africans because to do so would be to detract from the claim that whites can also be Africans with a right to territory in the continent. It would also occasion confusion in Afrikaans, since any translation of African into that language would be very close to the name Afrikaner. In the United States the struggle amongst Mexican-Americans over the most suitable name has been so vigorous that it has been referred to as 'the battle of the name'. Some prefer 'Spanish-speaking', others 'Americano', 'Latino', 'Hispano', or 'Chicano' (a diminutive of *mexicano*). There have even been disputes over whether Mexican-American should have a hyphen or not. The arguments reveal a lack of agreement within the group as to the nature of the group and its relation to United States society. To judge from the opinion polls and from the census, only a minority of those whom others would regard as Mexican-American identify themselves as such. The group designation 'Chicano', according to the surveys, is favoured by only 4 or 10 per cent of Mexican-Americans. Those who fought for its general adoption seem to have lost their battle of the name.

The Afro-American example has helped give rise to two separate battles of the name in Britain. They overlap and are often confused with one another, but there is advantage in distinguishing them. The first was one in which Afro-Caribbeans fought with themselves, or with the values with which they had been indoctrinated, and in favour of the self-referent 'black'. It was the argument that black could be as beautiful as white and that those who were black, rather than regretting it, should express black pride. For many Afro-Caribbeans, as for many Afro-Americans, the decision to identify themselves as black was the outcome of a personal struggle of great emotional significance. It testified to the depth of their previous psychological and cultural subordination. It has obvious parallels with the rejection of 'slave names' by Black Muslims in the United States, and with the adoption of African names. Younger blacks in Britain during the 1970s expressed considerable interest in a new religion that had originated in Jamaica according to which New World blacks were the people of Ras Tafari, the (former) Emperor of Ethiopia. This religion stressed their African identity and looked forward to the time when its adherents would escape from the new Babylon and return to Africa. It favoured African names. These movements reveal the significance of name-changing as a way in which individuals can change their identity and express that change. Those who in Britain fought a battle to call themselves black had won that battle by the mid 1970s.

The second battle has been the longer-running struggle to get official bodies and public institutions to use the name 'black' as a designation for all non-white persons. The outcome of this struggle is still uncertain, but the campaign for the inclusive use of the adjective has had many successes among the most articulate sections of the population. The main force behind the campaign must surely be a desire to mobilize the largest possible political constituency. It seems (a) to assume that the white–black boundary will not change; and then contend that (b) blacks must attain equality with whites in the distribution of privileges (income, wealth, positions of high prestige, etc.) and in the exercise of civil rights; with the result (c) that racial tension will then disappear.

As an argument in favour of an inclusive use of the name 'black', this overlooks a variety of objections. The failure of the attempt, in 1975–77, to create a national Black Peoples' Organization appears to have been due in part to the hesitations of Asian organizations and their objections to such a name. When, in 1982–83, the parliamentary Home Affairs Committee conducted hearings for its report, *Ethnic and Racial Questions in the Census*, the Chairman of the Commission for Racial Equality told its members: 'We would get major refusal if we were, as we do in our ordinary discussion groups, to refer to the Asian community as black' (HC 33, vol. II, p. 133). Younger Asians often differ from their elders on this point, but the historical experience of first-generation settlers from South Asia has been very different from that of Afro-Caribbeans. Though they come from cultural areas in which a light skin colour is preferred to a dark one, Asians have not been brought to hate their colour. In the localities in which they have settled there are often important tensions and prejudices between Asians and Afro-Caribbeans, while the social and political outlook of Asians is usually very different from that of those who maintain that they should identify themselves as blacks. The Muslims among them may wish to be classified by their religion rather than their colour. Discussion of such differences is sometimes represented as an attempt to divide and rule, but the differences will not be eliminated by pretending they do not exist. There is also evidence that white racial prejudice is expressed more strongly towards darker-skinned people and towards those whose other attributes indicate a lower social status, which shows that the various non-white groups have not suffered equally from white prejudice.

There are at least three reasons for not using black as a synonym for non-white. Firstly it can occasion uncertainty about which persons, apart from those of African or partly African origin, are being included. Despite its preference for this usage, the PSI study, *Black and White Britain*, has continually to distinguish data about employment, housing, education, etc., relating to Asians, from that relating to West Indians, because the figures show the circumstances of these two groups to be so different. Secondly, there is no reason to believe that a practice which encourages people to align themselves on either side of a single line of division promotes better racial relations. If boundaries remain firm and groups continually compare their incomes and experiences with others tension will not disappear. Thirdly, people who are of intermediate appearance, or who identify themselves with both black and white people according to circumstance, have a right to work out their identity and find a name or names acceptable to them; their options should not be restricted as if they were anomalies. As the history of Latin American countries shows, they can be a very important group. The objections to an inclusive use of 'black' apply to any similar use of 'white': it is inaccurate, emotionally-loaded and implies an over-simple division of the population. The best way to reduce racial tension is to attack the boundaries between groups by recognizing a variety of boundaries drawn in different places. Someone who identifies as a member of a particular group for one purpose does not then have to do so for other purposes; individual wishes and attributes can come before social stereotypes.

Chapter 5 described five steps taken by governments seeking to defend racial privilege which had the effect of increasing racial consciousness. In the United Kingdom the government has recently followed policies largely, but not altogether, contrary to these. It has legislated against the main forms of racial discrimination, imposing sanctions upon behaviour likely to support racial privilege (though it has been dilatory in remedying some technical deficiences in the drafting of the 1976 Act, slow to require firms bidding for government contracts to follow equal opportunities policies, and it could have responded more vigorously to the evidence about the incidence and serious nature of racial attacks since this has been available at least since 1981). To monitor the effectiveness of its policies it has approved a limited kind of racial classification (usually based on voluntary self-assignment). The collection of such statistics (e.g. about the proportion of employees in particular categories) draws attention in the short term to the very features which the policy seeks to make irrelevant in the long term; it increases racial consciousness and introduces an element of group competition. Not the least important is the fifth of the five steps. In Britain much of the inequality of opportunity to be found in one generation is transmitted to the next by a whole series of decisions affecting health, housing, education, employment, etc., which, though shaped by central government policies, are taken locally and are also affected by interpersonal relations.

CHAPTER 7
Conclusion

Revolutionaries usually start by trying to change the ways in which people feel about their societies. They seek to change popular consciousness. The extent to which they can do this depends upon the relationship between consciousness and social structure. There is an interaction between the way people feel about their society and the institutions of government, economy, religion, the mass media, and so on. Structure moulds consciousness but alterations in popular sentiment lead to changes in institutions. These changes reveal patterns of their own which can usefully be seen as social processes. Two particular processes were distinguished in Chapter 3 and illustrated in the chapters that followed. One process is that of group political action leading, for example, to the constitutional devices mentioned at the end of Chapter 4, and which are often designed to strike a new equilibrium between contending groups. The other process is that of individual change, for example, in the use of a language or in group affiliation. These processes interact with the structures, both modifying them and being modified by them. They interact similarly with consciousness, so consciousness, structure, and process constitute a kind of triangle.

Of the three points of this triangle, consciousness is the most difficult to study. How people feel about the various groups with which they identify themselves, and how they see the relations between these and other social units, varies from one context to another. So much depends upon the particular stimulus which causes an individual to align himself or herself socially. For example, the experience of travelling abroad and coming into contact with other peoples often has a profound effect in making individuals aware of features of their way of life which previously they had taken for granted. Until they meet others they may never have reflected upon ways in which their customs about meals, their norms of courtesy, their standards of dress, etc., were special to their own society. Only the discovery of other ways makes them conscious of their own. For a similar reason the revolutionary who wishes to awaken people to what he believes is a true consciousness of their position will publicize a conception of what the society could become if only people put their minds to it. The contrast between reality and what is believed to be a potentiality can be a stimulus to action. Consciousness is therefore often best studied by comparing the ways in which the same people behave in different contexts. For example, African governments have often deplored tribalism, meaning by this the tendency of their citizens to favour members of their own ethnic groups, to build ethnic parties, and to vote for candidates of similar ethnic origin to themselves. This the governments have seen as threatening national unity. What they have called tribalism is not something peculiar to countries with the kinds of ethnic groups referred to as tribes. It is not something peculiar to some people's mental processes. Tribalism is not a feature of life in regions inhabited by members of a single tribe, but a characteristic of cities and labour camps where people from different tribes meet in competition for jobs. The more intense the competition for scarce resources, the greater the stimulus for individuals to build groups of friends and allies who will help one another. Consciousness of tribe reflects the social context.

THE NATION-STATE

In world affairs today the prime structural unit influencing relations between people from different regions is the state. It has not always been so, for in earlier eras empires sprawled across large swathes of the globe. Popes and religious leaders were princes exercising political power. Many ethnic groups were untouched by either, but led independent lives trading with their neighbours and unaffected by the world outside. In the nineteenth century the map of Europe was changed by the rise of nationalism, a new consciousness which assumed that everyone had a nationality (expressed in language and culture but often identified with what the people of that period thought to be race). From this assumption the conclusion was drawn that everyone had the right to be governed with others of the same nationality as a distinctive state. The effect of the twentieth century's two world wars was to divide the world into some 160 states so that almost every bit of land belonged to some state. Formerly colonial territories, sometimes quite tiny ones, had, like others, to mould themselves on the European model of the nation-state. Often they were thrust into the competitive relations that generate a kind of international tribalism.

The need to organize and defend a common territory gives rise to a whole series of state institutions: to govern, to regulate an economy tied to a national currency, and to promote co-operation. These institutions maintain national distinctiveness. It is difficult to think of any three states which are as close to one another as Denmark, Norway, and Sweden. In international politics they form the core of a Nordic block. The peoples of the three countries feel strong bonds of alliance and at times an identity of interest, and yet in many other circumstances, like sport, they are great rivals. Their languages, like their state churches, are similar, but still different. Their children learn to identify with the histories of their own countries. Their economic interests (e.g. in respect of the European Community) are different. Danes, Norwegians, and Swedes will remain distinctive peoples as long as present international patterns continue.

Other groups seem set to retain their ethnic or national distinctiveness even though they do not control the states in which they live. Belgium is an area in which the French and Dutch cultures meet or overlap. The southern area of Walloonia is French-speaking, in the northern area of Flanders a dialect of Dutch, called Flemish, is spoken although for centuries the middle class in the North was French-speaking. In the 1920s class tensions in Flanders were expressed in a struggle over language use. Then after 1945 the economic development of Flanders was more rapid so that the Walloons felt left behind. Both groups felt threatened and aggrieved. Constitutional changes have given Flanders and Walloonia separate regional executives and legislatures. The central government has to include a fixed proportion of ministers from each community. These arrangements ensure a political equilibrium, but they lock citizens into a structure which maintains their ethnic distinctiveness.

Switzerland is similar, except that there citizenship depends upon membership of one of the twenty-five cantons or local communities. The cantons have the ultimate responsibility for the relief and welfare of those individuals who are on their registers. They have little incentive to add to their lists the names of migrant workers or their children. Within the cantons political animosities run deep.

Protestant and Catholic families often keep well apart. There are four national languages – German, French, Italian, and Romansh. Two-thirds of the Swiss speak *Schwyzerdütsch*, a dialect which turns them into a minority within the German-speaking world and gives them many of the touchy attitudes of other minority language speakers. So nearly everyone in Switzerland feels a member of a minority group. The country carries its commitment to democracy through to the local level. All legislation, whether federal or cantonal, can be altered if citizens demand a referendum. Since the political balance can change at central or local elections Swiss voters are always conscious of their group allegiances.

The people who constitute an ethnic group may be distinguished from their neighbours on many dimensions, yet it may happen that national identification gains importance at the expense of ethnic identification. An example of this process is provided by the Swedish-speaking group in western Finland. For some six centuries Finland was ruled by Swedes. Their language and culture dominated government, business, education, and the courts. Then in 1809 Sweden was forced to cede the territory to Russia, though the country continued to be administered by Swedish-speakers. A few weeks after the Bolshevik Revolution of 1917 the Finns declared their independence. Finnish and Swedish were proclaimed national languages and the administration made bilingual. Nevertheless there has been a steady decline in Swedish. According to the census of 1880 14.3 per cent of the population were Swedish-Finns; by 1920 it was 11.0 per cent and by 1975 6.4 per cent. The higher birth-rate of the Finnish-speakers is partly responsible for this. At present 44 communes are Swedish-speaking and 47 bilingual. Communes are obliged to provide primary schooling in the minority's language wherever there are at least 18 pupils. In 1978 6.3 per cent of a national sample stated that Swedish was their mother tongue, but 5.8 per cent gave it as their main language and only 4.8 per cent said that the language was used at their place of work. Though every facility has been given to the maintenance of the Swedish language and culture, it is declining because ethnic differences are not part of a competitive structure as in Belgium and Switzerland. The one locality which differs is the Åland Islands in the Gulf of Bothnia between the two states. There Swedish is dominant and the islanders have a special regional citizenship. Only people with this citizenship can acquire land or vote in communal or provincial elections. The islanders have special interests to preserve and, helped by their geographical location, they will doubtless preserve their Swedishness.

RELIGION

Groups with common territory organize to advance their interest in its resources. This must be considered the prime generator of group distinctiveness. The second has, for the last twenty centuries or so, been religion. In the Ottoman Empire (to which reference was made in Ch. 3) there was a *millet* system in which the religious leaders of ethnic minorities were held responsible for their communities (an arrangement which survives in modern Israel). Though members of these communities lived alongside one another for centuries they retained their distinctiveness. The power of religious differences to justify other kinds of difference is well illustrated in Northern Ireland, an area in which the British and Irish states meet and overlap. Catholic and Protestant leaders can agree in condemning terrorist actions. Nothing in either version of Christianity condones them, so in that sense the conflict is not religious. There is a political conflict over the division of resources within the province of Northern Ireland and over the relationship of the province to Britain and Ireland. The parties to the conflict are interest groups which are identified by religious institutions. They have, for example, attended separate Catholic and Protestant schools. The religious leaders of both groups can agree in condemning secularism. In their view of the world a religious faith must be the foundation of a person's social being. So in Northern Ireland almost everyone is accounted either a Catholic or Protestant regardless of whether he or she attends church or believes in the tenets of either faith. Everyone is shut into a religious classification which recognises no half-way house.

Some religious people regard their beliefs as personal, as belonging to a realm which should be free of state interference or regulation. It was to secure religious freedom that the earliest settlers went to North America, and they have been followed by others who wanted the same freedom. In the United States the organs of government are formally separate from matters of religion. They take no part in disputes about who shall speak on behalf of a faith or what demands may be made in its name. Seen from an international perspective this is an unusual position for a government to adopt. Elsewhere people of strong religious belief have demanded that their governments act to support and extend the true faith. Several states now proclaim themselves Islamic republics. Many have state churches. Not all states can agree that the right to freedom of religion includes a person's right to change his or her religion.

In England and Wales, the 1944 Education Act requires that

schools conduct a daily act of collective worship and provide religious education. Religious schools can qualify for financial support from the government. The Committee of Inquiry into the Education of Children from Ethnic Minority Groups chaired by Lord Swann, recommended in 1985 that this be reviewed 'given the multiplicity of beliefs now present in society' and 'in favour of a non-denominational and undogmatic approach to religious education'. The government rejected this recommendation. In 1986 a local authority in London recommended public support for a fundamentalist Islamic primary school. Leading figures associated with the National Secular Society protested. Soon, they said, there would be proposals for Sikh, Hindu, and other schools. Children attending them would be isolated from the wider society. Self-segregation would build up a greater animosity even than that seen in Northern Ireland. People have a right to combine and establish private schools, but they should not be able to claim financial support from the public purse. Therefore Parliament should phase out all subsidies to denominational schools. In reply it was said that most denominational schools do not set out to indoctrinate their children with sectarian beliefs, and that they should not lose their status on account of the activities of a small minority. Since secular ideas had not improved the moral standards of the society, taking religion out of the schools would not be a progressive step. This debate will surely continue because a distinctive religion helps a minority to cohere and to exert group pressure.

The proportion of the white British population who attend church regularly or are more than nominally Christian has fallen dramatically during the twentieth century. The secularizing trend has been accelerated by the weakening of local communities, by the growth of scientific explanation, and by the market economy. In modern industrial society the major forces bringing about cultural change are those which derive from the opportunities for producers to derive profit from providing goods and services which consumers purchase. Other powerful pressures are generated by mass entertainment, popular music, spectator sports, and other activities in which the consumer calls the tune. The mass is an aggregate of individuals, who share common tastes in varying and changing degrees. Many of these tastes are shared by people of different religion and different ethnic origin. The pursuit of consumer satisfaction often weakens the bonds of religious or ethnic community.

That racial differences should remain so important in the United States and South Africa may, from this standpoint, seem exceptional.

Afro-Americans occupy distinctive territories within United States cities, but they do not control them in the way that a state can control its territory. They cannot build institutions comparable to those of a state. Afro-Americans are the oldest of the minorities in their country and, despite some features of speech, food preferences, and music (which are sometimes copied by members of other groups) they are in some ways the most American of the minorities. Some sociologists, like William Julius Wilson, contend that class differences among Afro-Americans have increased substantially, blunting the effect of racial differences. Well-to-do blacks and poor blacks combine politically because it is to their common advantage to create as big a national constituency as possible, because they remember their common history of oppression, and because they sympathize with one another's struggles. Yet the economic basis for such an alliance is being reduced. In South Africa, where the various groups differed in language, religion, and culture as well as race, they have moved closer to one another: in learning one another's languages, in playing the same sports, watching the same television programmes, and employing (even if in very unequal degree) the same technology. The processes of change which would otherwise have altered the social structure, have diversified people's interests and modified their social consciousness, have been held in check by the government's scheme for distributing privilege. It highlights racial differences because these differences are used to structure interest groups.

IMMIGRATION

As Chapter 6 has shown, racial consciousness may also be important in situations of immigration. Individuals enter another country in search of economic betterment and come there to constitute ethnic and racial minorities. They are then subject to processes of change as one generation succeeds the next. Studies in the United States of the settlement of immigrants from Europe have pointed up differences in the outlook of the first three generations. The experience of the first generation includes special kinds of excitement and pain. On the one hand is the excitement of new opportunities that often stimulate members of the first generation to work particularly hard to provide security for their families. The pain arises because they have learned in their countries of origin values which are rejected in their new country. This is particularly relevant to relations between parents and children. The immigrants have frequently come from societies in which great respect is shown towards elderly kinsfolk, and they expect similar respect in their turn as they grow older. Their children, however, have to make their way with their peers in the new society and they often spurn their parent's exhortations as old-fashioned and irrelevant. So in many immigrant communities there is a struggle, as parents seek to maintain central elements of their culture and to resist what they see as the corrupting influence of the majority culture.

To judge from the American studies, the second generation is usually fairly successful in going its own way and forcing their parents to recognize that the customs of the new country must dominate. For this generation the school and the peer group have set the standards as to how a good American should behave. This must account for the tremendous pressure to conform to peer group expectations which all children still experience in United States schools. The pain of the second generation lies in the feeling of guilt that they have been too harsh in reacting against their parents' ideas. In the third generation this burden is lifted and young people often wish to return to their 'roots', finding out about their grandparents' origins and sometimes identifying with their ethnicity, secure that they are not the less American for doing so. This sequence led Marcus Lee Hansen, a historian of Swedish settlement in North America, to formulate what has been called Hansen's law: 'What the son wishes to forget, the grandson wishes to remember.' This proposition embodies a valuable insight, but it cannot be treated as valid for all minorities. In some cities of the north-east of the United States political parties have sought to ensure that their slate of candidates always included one name of each of the locally numerous minorities, so there might be one Irish, one Italian, and one Jewish name. When ethnicity was built into the political structure in this way, and when relatively cheap air flights provided a way in which groups could keep in touch with their communities of origin, there was less reason for the second generation to react against their parents' ideas.

The children of Irish and Italian settlers in the United States have often married fellow Catholics of different ethnic parentage. An increasing proportion of young Jewish people have married Gentiles and ceased to observe the Jewish religion. So in successive generations individuals have had ancestors of varied ethnicity and could identify themselves with one or more ethnic groups or none at all. Distinctive ethnic communities have usually dissolved by the third generation. This experience may contain lessons for those members of New Commonwealth minorities in Britain who hope that their cultural

127

distinctiveness can be preserved. The evidence suggests that a group can maintain cultural distinctiveness for more than three generations when for religious reasons it follows a self-segregating communal way of life based upon agricultural production. The notable examples are the Amish communities of Pennsylvania and some similar groups in other parts of America. About one in four of their children eventually leave these communities but, since their birthrate is high, they have been expanding in population. Their way of life is based upon a rejection of modern technology, of education beyond the eighth grade (about 14 years) and of the materialistic values of an industrial culture. Their distinctive costume means that if they take their horse and buggy to drive in a neighbouring town, they stand out as very different from the majority. Many features combine to reinforce the division between them and others. Another group which has succeeded in maintaining its distinctiveness for an even longer period is that of the Gypsies. Though they have distinctive beliefs about pollution, their culture is not so very different from that of non-Gypsies, except for their moving from place to place which restricts their children's schooling, and, because of the circumstances in which it is done, attracts the hostility of non-Gypsies. That hostility is not altogether unwelcome to Gypsy parents because it helps bind their children to the group's way of life and discourages them from seeing opportunities in the wider society. They live on the fringes of industrial society, collecting scrap metal, laying tarmac, and undertaking seasonal work like berry-picking.

Hitherto only Jews have sustained an ethnic distinctiveness while living within the heart of such societies. Their success is attributable in part to a religion which tells them they are the chosen people and which is practised in a distinctive language. For nearly 2,000 years they have been a people without a homeland, so that if they were to follow the dictates of their religion they had to do this as a minority wherever they found themselves. The foundation of the state of Israel in 1948 changed that. In every generation Jewish communities have lost some of their members who have ceased to identify themselves as Jews. In the United States the proportion who do this seems to be increasing significantly. Those who wish to identify as Jews may in future be under more pressure to go to Israel if they are to feel fully Jewish, and in such circumstances their identity will become more national and less religious.

A review of the history of minorities therefore suggests that no ethnic group can maintain its cultural distinctiveness for more than three generations unless either:

(a) it controls its own territory; or
(b) enjoys rights protected by the state's constitution; or
(c) is so large that it can prevent any other group enforcing upon it an unacceptable policy; or
(d) its members are content not to claim all the rights of citizenship in the state in which they live; or
(e) its members are committed to a distinctive religion, preferably one which requires that worship be conducted in a language peculiar to the group.

This does not mean, however, that it may not be desirable to assist minorities to retain their cultures by providing financial assistance to community enterprises, or by arranging extra tuition in minority languages. Multicultural policies in education can help all pupils better appreciate that peoples in other cultures see international affairs from a different standpoint. They can ease the pressures upon ethnic minority children to conform to majority expectations. Such policies can be justified by short-term considerations and do not depend upon any particular assumptions about the direction of long-term change.

Social minorities are able to maintain their distinctiveness over the generations when they can differentiate themselves on more than one dimension. This has to be related to the discussion in Chapter 1 of the many-stranded quality of interpersonal relations. Two individuals may be able to define the relation between them as a business relationship, or a gender relationship, or a racial relationship. One might wish to define it as a racial relationship and the other think this inappropriate. An example can be taken from the study of black–white relations in Mississippi in the 1930s referred to on p. 75. There it is reported that a lower-class white woman pointed a pistol at a respectable black professional man; he knocked it from her hand. She ran down one of the main business streets of a fairly small country town shouting 'That nigger struck me!' (i.e. she represented it as an offence against racial norms). The woman succeeded in getting the black man arrested, but the judge refused to regard it as a matter of race and dismissed the charge (Davis *et al.* 1941: 477). The judge had the power to declare that the woman's definition of the relation was wrong. In the past white officials often used their power to define situations racially when there were good grounds for not doing so.

Since then there has been a change. In situations in which a racial minority is disadvantaged members of the majority may be inclined to believe that the cause of the disadvantage is not majority discrimination but, say, the relatively recent arrival of the minority.

129

Racial consciousness

Representatives of the minority may argue for a racial definition. A very practical example of this is the recording of racial attacks in Britain. When attention was first drawn to this matter the police were reluctant to classify a reported attack by a white man on, say, an Asian man, as racial. They were inclined to argue that there could be other grounds for such an attack and that it was not to be so classified unless there were good grounds for concluding that the attacker was racially motivated. By the very nature of the circumstances in which attacks occurred it was very difficult to assemble such evidence. More recently the police have been instructed to count as racial any incident which appears to the investigating officer to include an element of racial motivation or which includes an allegation of racial motivation made by any person.

The case of racial attacks is relatively straightforward in that everyone can see the need to collect figures about their frequency and to investigate reports, but there are other circumstances in which racial definition is problematic. One of the reasons some members of the minorities were opposed to the introduction of a racial question into the 1981 census, as mentioned in Chapter 1, was that they feared they might be racially classified in circumstances to which such a classification was inappropriate. Racial consciousness is not reduced by simply forbidding racial classification. It is reduced by social processes which change structures so that more and more relationships are conducted on a non-racial basis. It is processes of this kind which weaken the distinctiveness of minorities.

RACIAL EQUALITY

Any discussion of the changing of structures must raise the question of racial equality and how this objective is best defined. On p. 105 equality was defined in factual terms; it was said that the number 5 is not equal to the number 6 and that in the army the pay of a private is not equal to that of a major. Differentials in reward are necessary in any organization as incentives for promotion, especially when this entails moving house (and uprooting the family) in order to work in another branch of the concern. Differentials periodically require adjustment to respond to changes in the demand for and supply of qualified personnel. The basic conception of equality as a moral value is that of equality before the law. It can be expressed as the principle of non-discrimination which now features in the international human rights conventions: no one shall be treated unequally on grounds of sex, age, wealth, race, colour, or ethnic origin. Nor shall there be any discrimination in any selection of individuals for jobs, promotion, or any other kind of privilege.

If the figures show that there are no army majors from a particular ethnic group this is not necessarily proof that racial equality has not been attained in that field. In India, the Sikhs have a reputation as soldiers and a distinguished military record, whereas Gujerati culture does not value military service. Some groups, like the Amish, are opposed to it on conscientious grounds. However, if the figures showed that a disproportionate number of applicants from a group were being rejected or that, after allowing for the time needed to achieve promotion, the number of majors from a particular group was not proportionate to the number of privates, this might indeed be evidence of discrimination and therefore of a falling short from the standard of equal treatment. This view of the matter takes no account of the inter-generational transmission of inequality discussed in Chapter 5. Some individuals are born into privilege, others into deprivation. There are great inequalities in their early years, in diet, health care, schooling, and in the circumstances which encourage ambition, resilience, and the ability to persevere. Children are ready to admire certain adults as heroes and heroines; these serve as role models, as figures upon whom they can model themselves and who set standards as to what they may hope to attain for themselves. There will, therefore, be differences in the social development of those children who can identify with the people at the top of their society, and those who cannot. Racial equality is not attained until these sources of disadvantage have been overcome.

There are two possible routes towards racial equality. One is the destruction of racial categories by permitting or encouraging an increase in the number of people of an intermediate appearance so that differences of complexion follow a continuous distribution as in Fig. 3.1(b) and (d). This route has been followed in parts of Latin America, though far from perfectly. There is still substantial inequality (more, indeed, than in most of Europe), but it is, for the most part, an inequality of individuals rather than of groups. The second route is that of preserving racial categories but of intervening in economic and social affairs to promote an equality of results. It is said that there will be racial peace only when there is racial equality and that this, in a society divided into black and white, means that the average black income must be as high as the average white income. The two groups must be roughly equal on all important measures.

131

The proportion for black and white legislators, judges, doctors, engineers, and so on must correspond to their proportions in the total population. This conception of equality (which is common in the United States) appeals to minority politicians because the preservation of racial categories safeguards their special constituencies. But so long as relations are structured in terms of group competition there is no reason to expect that the achievement of statistical equality would lead to a reduction in tension. Constant questioning about 'How are we doing now?' or 'Are we still equal on that measure?' would reinforce group consciousness and keep alive the sense of racial membership. The experience of societies divided by language (like Belgium), and religion (like Northern Ireland) suggests that continuous 'us and them' comparisons generate pressures towards partition rather than unity.

In the long run, the first route offers the better way of overcoming social distinctions based upon differences irrelevant to the moral deserts of individuals. Yet the power of transmitted inequality is so great in an industrial society that racial distinctions cannot be overcome by simply declaring them irrelevant. To promote equality of opportunity it is sometimes necessary to try to reduce inequalities of results. People should be free to be unequal if they wish, but that freedom can be limited by stereotypes derived from the success or lack of success of people assigned to the same group. In the short run, therefore, it is important not to turn a blind eye to the way that physical differences are used to preserve inequalities.

In Chapter 3 the difference between Latin America and the United States was represented as a contrast between a pattern of individual change captured by the concept of assimilation, and a pattern of group bargaining reflected in a concept of equilibrium. In the first pattern the boundary between the groups was soft, so that memberships could change and the composition of groups alter. In the second pattern the boundary was hard and the composition of the groups changed only slowly. The position in Britain shows some of the characteristics of each of these patterns. Group relations are dynamic in that they are influenced by a multitude of forces pulling in different directions; the overall system of relations could move closer to either the Latin American or the United States pattern, or, indeed, establish some new pattern. The sources of change are twofold. On the one hand British society is influenced by international economic and political developments, including technological advances. On the other hand, members of the majority and minority groups seek their own advantage by both individual and group activity. When they feel that their interests are served by aligning themselves with an ethnic group, a racial category, or a class that crosses racial lines, then they are likely to combine with others. This then reinforces any ideas they may have about their naturally belonging in such a group. So racial consciousness increases or decreases. Differences in appearance do not of themselves give rise to social groups. It is the use people make of such differences to identify themselves with some in opposition to others that determines the strength and the nature of racial consciousness.

Students' appendix

CHAPTER 1

A reading of this chapter should lead you to reflect upon the circumstances in which you are most and least conscious of racial differences, and what it is that triggers off your awareness. It should also lead you to start noticing what words the people round you use to designate people of other groups. Is there a difference between older and younger generations? Is there a difference between the words used in your locality and those employed in TV programmes? Are people of other groups identified by their colour, their nationality, or the locality in which they reside?

You should be able to say how you would set about drafting a question concerning racial and ethnic identification for use in a census; or for use in a form for monitoring appointments to see if the proportion of persons in various racial categories appointed to particular kinds of job corresponds to their proportion in the wider society. The best discussion is that contained in *Ethnic and Racial Questions in the Census* (HC 33) plus the two volumes of evidence. This is a report of the House of Commons Home Affairs Committee, Subcommittee on Race Relations and Immigration, for the session 1982–83. A brief account of the difficulties can be found in Banton (1985). The journal of the Commission for Racial Equality, *New Community*, 1980, nos 1 and 2, is a special issue containing a collection of articles on this problem. There are related articles in other issues of this journal, notably White (1979) which analyses problems of nomenclature systematically; Bulmer (1980) is an informative rejoinder.

A reading of this chapter should also have led you to conclude that some apparent disagreements in arguments about racial relations derive from a failure to define the terms that are being used. These relations are very complex and therefore require a complex vocabulary if they are to be properly described. One way of reducing potential disagreement is to get maximum clarity about the reasons for raising a topic. The question 'What are good racial relations?' can give rise to lengthy discussion without coming to any definite conclusion, yet everyone might agree upon what in practice would constitute an improvement to a particular situation. It is possible that a sociologist's view will differ from the views of people for whom inter-racial contacts are a matter of daily experience. It is also worth while pausing over the way in which conflict may be differentiated from other forms of struggle, the distinction between constructive and destructive conflict, and the idea of positive-sum, negative-sum, and zero-sum games; game theory is now being used in all the social sciences.

CHAPTER 2

The first chapter drew attention to the problems of classifying people in everyday life and the names given to the resulting categories. This chapter has taken one of those words and shown how its meaning has changed and expanded over the past 400 years. The best way to understand the many senses of the word 'race' is to learn how and why it has been used in new ways. For Britain, a useful book is Walvin (1971) which reprints some documents that are difficult to locate in their original form. There is widespread misunderstanding about the influence of the slave-trade upon British ideas of race; by far the best treatment of this subject is to be found in Barker (1978), but it is a dense and detailed study that deserves to be read slowly. For the nineteenth century, Lorimer (1978) can be recommended, but this, too, is a book based on a doctoral thesis and not an introductory work.

You should understand the historical contexts within which ideas about race took shape, while appreciating that there was an independent growth in scientific knowledge about the causes of phenotypical variation. There were three main phases. In the eighteenth century the dominant view was that all humans were descended from Adam and Eve; environmental differences were thought to account for the appearance of racial differences. The second phase, in which racial differences were considered permanent, culminated in the doctrine of racial typology. The third phase, inaugurated by Darwin, has led to the creation of genetics and to a revolution in the understanding of biology. These three phases are summarized in Banton (1983a: 34-50) while Banton and Harwood (1975) offers a more elementary exposition both of the history and of modern scientific knowledge concerning differences in culture, behaviour, and measured intelligence. For blood groups Mourant (1983) is useful, but you may prefer to look for an introductory account in a textbook of human biology.

The reader will doubtless reflect upon the significance of new words. Were there racial relations in the period before there was a word 'race'? What difference may the availability of the word have made to interpersonal relations? Was 'race' actually used or did people designate groups by colour, country of origin, or religion? Unfortunately, the historical evidence is scanty. The development of racial consciousness depends upon there being words to express and mould that consciousness. Words that are introduced by scholars and scientists have to be popularized if they are to affect that consciousness. This is also true of the word 'racism'. You should be able to differentiate the use of this word in any sociological context in which it is given a technical meaning from its meaning in popular argument. Sometimes racism is used as a concept, and sometimes as an epithet to disparage or stigmatize something or someone. The art and language of persuasive speaking is called rhetoric, and there is a rhetoric of racial relations in which speakers utilize those words which best enable them to project their interpretations. This rhetoric takes different forms depending upon the viewpoint advanced, but a common feature is that of concealing the assumptions which underlie the words chosen. Consider again the different definitions in the UN debate about Zionism. Whether Zionism is or is not a form of racism depends upon the definition of the key terms. On occasion racism has been defined in such a way that only white people can display it. One of sociology's contributions is to clarify the vocabulary of discussion about the various kinds of social relations.

CHAPTER 3

The previous chapter introduced the idea of variation. This one explains the difference between continuous and discontinuous variation. When you read the first two chapters did you assume that racial variation was discontinuous? Does your understanding of continuous variation cause you to modify any ideas you may have held about race? Can you use it to explain the frequency of blood group B in different parts of Europe?

For further information on the different kinds of classification that developed in North, Central, and South America, see Banton (1983a: 15–31). A helpful account of the way in which the concept of equilibrium can be used in sociology is to be found in Homans (1950: 281–312).

The distortion of the concept of assimilation has given it a bad name, so that those who are concerned to describe a goal for social policy more frequently write of integration as 'a process by which diverse elements are combined into a unity while retaining their basic identity', or of pluralism as one which 'aims at uniting different ethnic groups in a relation of mutual interdependence'. These are quotations from a UN special study in 1971 which also stated 'based on the idea of the superiority of the dominant culture, assimilation aims at the achievement of homogeneity within the State by ensuring that groups discard their cultures in favour of the dominant culture'. In this book assimilation is used to mean 'becoming similar' without any assumption of superiority and without equating it with absorption. It is also worth noting that UN bodies have been trying for over thirty-six years to agree upon a definition of 'minority', so far without success (see Thornberry 1987:3–4). The difficulty is that minorities are assumed to be populations which deserve special protection from the state whereas governments, for political reasons, do not want to assume any special obligations towards them. The simplest solution is to use the word in a numerical sense and regard any set of persons who are less than half the population as a minority. This can then be qualified by saying whether it is a racial or a political or a religious or a linguistic minority, etc.

After studying this chapter you should have an understanding of racial consciousness as something that is manifested by individuals because they are members of groups and subject to group influences. One of sociology's major problems is to account for the interaction between the individual and society. You should now be able to show how racial consciousness is a product of that interaction. Individual change (as by the learning of a new language or the loss of an old one) is usually the result of a series of small decisions, but they are made in a social context. Group changes (like those which occur when the members of one group try to establish a new intergroup equilibrium) are possible only because of pressure from individuals. If one group fails to initiate change, or loses ground because the other succeeds, that shows how the social structure restricts the alternatives available to individuals.

CHAPTER 4

The writer who has pioneered the analysis of the processes discussed in this chapter is Leo Kuper. Writing at times in collaboration with M. G. Smith, he propounded a conception of the plural society as one in which political relations influence relations to the means of production more than any influence in the opposite direction (for a summary, see Banton 1983a: 91-4). He applied this to the analysis of revolutions in Zanzibar, Rwanda, Burundi, and Algeria, sometimes drawing parallels with South Africa (Kuper 1977). He then went on to the analysis of the processes which lead to and make possible genocide (Kuper 1981) and cast a spotlight upon the relative ineffectiveness of the United Nations and other international organizations in preventing abuses by member states (Kuper 1985). Students of racial relations have been slow to see the significance for their studies of international organizations and the development of international law (on which see the excellent introduction, Sieghart 1986). A useful digest of Kuper's later work is available in his 1982 Minority Rights Group report. For information about the massacres in Rwanda and Burundi the best source is another report (Lemarchand and Martin 1974) published by the same body (which has its headquarters at 29 Craven Street, London, WC2N 5NT).

This chapter has given you further examples of the ways in which large-scale social processes (in particular the material superiority of European states stemming from the adoption of a capitalist economy) can structure the kinds of relations possible between people belonging to different racial groups. It has shown that a desire for political dominance can transform relations between groups of people of the same colour into bitter and bloody conflict. It should stimulate you to think what relation, if any, there has been between racial ideology and imperialism. How would you set about determining the racial consciousness of whites in Zimbabwe prior to its independence? How might it differ from Nigeria where whites were a much smaller minority? It is important to consider what sort of information is needed to answer questions of this kind before looking to see if the information is available. Remember, too, that imperial rule often entailed the introduction of people of a third racial group: Indians in Africa, Chinese in Malaysia, Indians in Fiji, etc.

Such questions can be linked with the discussion of constitutional provisions at the end of the chapter. It is constitutions which prescribe who may vote, what the legislature may do (whether for example, it may pass laws that prevent an immigrant minority purchasing land, as in Fiji). They regulate citizenship (in Sierra Leone, for example, citizenship is restricted 'to persons of Negro African descent'). The constitution and the law determine the kinds of relations into which people from different groups may enter. They may prevent conflict and they may provoke it. They attempt to secure an equilibrium.

CHAPTER 5

No reader should have difficulty locating histories of the United States and South Africa to fill out what is written here. Encyclopaedia articles can also be helpful. For chapter-length summaries which concentrate on the aspects most relevant to racial relations, and indicate the sources used here, refer to Banton (1983a: 209–84). After reading the chapter you should be in a position to draw up a balance sheet with respect to the first three of the steps for maintaining a caste-like structure (classification, segregation, sanctions) to show the anticipated benefits that led to their adoption and the costs that were entailed. The story of a very untypical community in Cape Town by Watson (1970) brings out these issues on the local level. A very readable account of the present situation in South Africa that illustrates the implications of economic changes for the daily lives of black South Africans can be found in Lelyveld (1986). The proposition that when people compete as individuals this dissolves racial boundaries, whereas when they compete as groups this reinforces them, is elaborated in Banton (1983a: 104 *et seq*). The inter-generational transmission of inequality is discussed in many sociology textbooks but Atkinson, Maynard, and Trinder (1983) furnish up-to-date detail. The question to consider is how racial differences may influence a pre-existing social pattern.

After studying the chapter you should be able to explain why the steps taken by the superordinate racial group increase racial consciousness in the subordinate group. The people in the B group feel deprived relative to those in the P group once they come to appreciate that the differences are not facts of nature but the outcome of social (including political and economic) relations. Religion may be important to this awakening if it stresses the moral equality of an alternative kind of society. Read the Old Testament book of Daniel 11: 11-15, and think how they might have appeared to Afro-Americans before the Civil War between North and South! An excellent, though now somewhat dated, account of the Black Muslim movement in the United States can be found in Essien-Udom (1962). The classic study of comparable religious movements among black South Africans is that by Sundkler (1961). Though the independent black churches are important in South Africa because of the size of their congregations, they are not now the vehicle for a revolutionary consciousness that once they were.

CHAPTER 6

Hitherto the decennial census in England and Wales has not included any questions about race or ethnicity. It has been possible to infer these to some degree from the tables about birthplace, but as more persons of New Commonwealth parentage have been born in Britain it has become preferable to use figures from sample surveys like the *Labour Force Survey* and the *National Dwelling and Household Survey*. In the former, subjects are given a card and asked 'to which of the groups on the card do you consider that you belong?' and the question is repeated for other members of the household. Statistics deriving from such studies are brought up to date in government publications like *Key Data*, *Social Trends*, and *Population Trends*.

From Table 6.2 you should be able to prepare a set of histograms, or block diagrams, comparing the age structure of the various groups. Table 6.1 will enable you to prepare another set to show the proportions in each group who have been resident in Britain for different lengths of time. You will need first to express these figures as percentages. Note that whereas the census tables for England and Wales, and those for Scotland, are presented separately, this is a table for Great Britain. Great Britain is the sum of England, Wales, and Scotland. The United Kingdom consists of Great Britain plus Northern Ireland.

The first PEP/PSI study of racial discrimination was described in Daniel (1968), the second in Smith (1977), and the third in Brown (1984). There have been many smaller studies of discrimination in the recruitment to jobs, the allocation of council houses, the price paid for private houses, etc. They should remind you of one of sociology's chief lessons: to interpret the findings of any study it is essential to examine the methods by which those findings were obtained. In general you should find the annual reports of the Commission for Racial Equality particularly helpful. They contain summaries of cases brought under the 1976 Act, brief accounts of the commission's researches, and lists of its publications. With respect to court cases you should ask yourself about the case brought against Gwynedd County Council. Had it succeeded, would it have been an example of direct or indirect discrimination? Note that under the 1976 Act someone who suffers racial discrimination has a remedy by way of civil proceedings, whereas incitement to racial hatred is a criminal offence. You could be prosecuted for incitement but not for discrimination. On racial attacks see the important report of the House of Commons Home Affairs Committee, *Racial Attacks and Harassment*, 1985–86, HC 409. For the way questions of immigration and racial relations have been handled on the political scene see Layton-Henry (1984). A good account of the urban riots of 1980–81 can be found in Kettle and Hodges (1982) while Benyon (1986) offers a succinct review of the various explanations which have been advanced. Do not generalize about alienation without having studied Gaskell and Smith (1981). The same authors have also compared two possible explanations for the hostility of young blacks towards the police (Gaskell and Smith 1984).

A book containing a helpful series of essays describing different racial and ethnic minorities settled in Britain has been edited by Watson (1977). For a monograph on the Sikhs, Helweg (1979) can be recommended. A useful short review of the Rastafarian religion among West Indians is Cashmore (1984). If you wish to follow up the contrasts in the strategies followed by West Indian and South Asian minorities, an essay which can be specially recommended is that by Rex (1982). Concerning children of mixed origin there is a pioneering study by Wilson (1987); some would consider the use of race in its title to be unfortunate. For a collection of articles about multicultural education you may find Whitaker (1983) useful.

After reading this chapter you should be ready to reflect upon some of the issues raised in Chapter 1. You may yourself have strong views on the best names for different groups or know people who do. You should now be able to give a better explanation of why group names are often thought so important; why in everyday life groups are defined in ways appropriate to everyday problems; why in designing a social survey stricter definitions are necessary to see that subjects are classified unambiguously using names acceptable to them; and why for sociological purposes it is necessary to try and develop analytical concepts which are independent of popular consciousness.

CHAPTER 7

By now you will be aware both of the importance of racial consciousness and the difficulty of studying it systematically. The racial component can never be abstracted completely from other features of a person's outlook. One way of approaching the problem is by studying cross-identification. A class of pupils in a London school could be asked to imagine that they are watching a boxing match between a white boxer from Glasgow and a black boxer from London. How many of the white pupils would identify with the boxer from Glasgow because he is white? Using this technique it is possible to vary racial identities and situations to test the strength of racial consciousness compared with national or class consciousness.

You should also by now be alert to elements of majority–minority relations which are common to several countries and to some of the contrasts. For the comparison of Belgium, Switzerland, and Finland see Palley (1986) and for Northern Ireland, Jackson, (1984). A fuller discussion of the Amish, Gypsies, and Jews as resisting assimilation is in Banton (1983a: 153–64). A film entitled *Witness!* gives an impression of life inside an Amish community. How the Japanese have prevented their minorities assimilating can be learned from De Vos *et al.* (1983). Common features in the social psychology of minorities are brought out in Tajfel (1978).

The pressures that bear upon second-generation members of racial minorities in Britain are different from the pressures to assimilate which in the United States affected the immigrants from Europe and resulted in Hansen's law. You should be able to work out the main differences. For an entertaining novel which shows how West Indian men in London could find their new opportunities exciting and pleasurable, see Selvon (1956). Discussions of the appropriate policies for majority-minority relations in Britain usually turn upon (a) measures to reduce discrimination and promote equality; (b) the extent to which minority groups should be recognized as distinct groups requiring their own representation. This chapter has cast doubt upon the chances of such groups maintaining their distinctiveness for more than three generations. You should now be able to discuss the issues in terms of consciousness, structure, and process; the variables of territory, constitutional rights, and relative size are structural features; the commitment of minority members to their own groups and their adoption of the majority's values can be discussed in terms of process, since they change more rapidly than the structural features. You should understand relations in Britain the better for having formed a view of the long-term possibilities.

Glossary

Assimilation The process of becoming similar.

Colour tax Price differential paid by persons of a different colour to obtain services of a quality similar to those obtained by persons not subject to discrimination.

Ethnic group A category of persons constituted by self-identification in terms of common descent and culture.

Ethnocentrism The tendency to evaluate matters by reference to the values shared in the subject's own ethnic group as if that group were the centre of everything.

Genocide Action intended to destroy, in whole or in part, a national, ethnic, racial, or religious group as such.

Incitement to racial hatred Publication (in speech or writing) of words threatening, abusive, or insulting to members of a racial group with either the intention or the likely effect of stirring up hatred against them.

Phenotype The phenotype is the outward appearance of an organism (like a human being). It may be paired with the concept of genotype, denoting the underlying genetic constitution of the organism.

Positive action (miscalled positive discrimination) Affording training and similar facilities to members of a racial group to enable them to compete on an equal basis with others for employment.

Prejudice An emotional and rigidly unfavourable attitude towards members of a given group.

Race 1. A set of people of common descent (race as lineage) (1570).*
2. A set of people with a distinctive nature (race as type) (1800).
3. A set of people with common characters (race as subspecies) (1859).

144

4. A set of people distinguished by the frequency of one or more genes (race as population) (1950).

Racial category   A set defined by a popular assumption that people of a particular appearance belong together, are likely to behave in distinctive ways, and in some circumstances should be treated differently.

Racial disadvantage   Any form of handicap associated with assignment to a racial group.

Racial discrimination   The unfavourable treatment of persons on racial grounds. Racial discrimination may be either categorical or statistical. In the former all members of a category are presumed to share the characteristics which evoke discrimination. In the latter discrimination occurs because a high proportion of people in that category are believed to have these characteristics. In law, racial discrimination is either direct or indirect. Direct discrimination may be equated with categorical discrimination; it is less favourable treatment on racial grounds. Indirect discrimination may be unintentional and may not arise from racial grounds; it occurs when someone imposes on another a condition which:

(a) is such that the proportion of persons of the same social group as that other who can comply with it is considerably smaller than the proportion of persons not of that racial group who can comply with it; and

(b) he cannot show to be justifiable irrespective of the colour, race, nationality, or ethnic or national origin of the person to whom it is applied; and

(c) is to the detriment of that other because he cannot comply with it.

Racial equality   This may be defined either factually (as an absence of racial disadvantage) or morally (as a belief that no one shall be treated unequally on grounds of race or colour).

Racial group   A category of persons defined in racial terms by non-members (not necessarily a social group).

Racial relations   Relations in which behaviour is racially motivated. When a man defines someone as belonging in a racial category other than his own, he regards that person as having rights and obligations in some way different from those of a person belonging to the same racial category as himself.

Racism   1. The doctrine that race determines culture (1933).

2. The use of racial beliefs and attitudes to subordinate and control a category of people defined in racial terms (1967).

3. A historical complex, generated within capitalism, facilitating the exploitation of categories of people defined in racial terms (1970).

4. Anything connected with racial discrimination (1980).

Relations The behaviour between two individuals, who may interact in accordance with one or more sets of role expectations.

Relationship The behaviour expected of persons occupying two paired roles (e.g. landlord–tenant).

Role The expected behaviour associated with a social position. The concept is usually employed in circumstances in which one role is paired with another (e.g. father–daughter) or related to others in an organization (e.g. manager–foreman–machinist).

Social distance Social acceptability in relationships of varying intimacy.

* Dates following an entry indicate either the first published use of the word in the sense used or the date when it started to be used in the sense.

Bibliography

Aberbach, Joel D., and Walker, Jack L. (1970) The meanings of Black Power: a comparison of white and black interpretations of a political slogan, *American Political Science Review* 64: 367-88.

Anwar, Muhammad (1986) *Race and Politics: ethnic minorities and the British political system*. London: Tavistock.

Atkinson, A. B., Maynard, A. K., and Trinder, C. G. (1983). *Parents and Children: incomes in two generations*. London: Heinemann.

Banton, Michael (1983a) *Racial and Ethnic Competition*. Cambridge: Cambridge University Press.

Banton, Michael (1983b) The influence of colonial status upon black-white relations in England, 1948-58, *Sociology* 17: 546-59.

Banton, Michael (1985) Racial classification in the census, *Social Studies Review* 1(1): 21-5.

Banton, Michael, and Harwood, Jonathan (1975) *The Race Concept*. Newton Abbott: David and Charles.

Barker, Anthony J. (1978) *The African Link: British attitudes to the Negro in the era of the African slave trade, 1550-1807*. London: Frank Cass.

Benyon, John (1986) Turmoil in the cities, *Social Studies Review* 1(3): 3-8.

Blumenbach, Johann Friedrich (1865) *The Anthropological Treatises of Johann Friedrich Blumenbach*. London: Anthropological Society of London.

Boyd, William C. (1950) *Genetics and the Races of Man*. Boston: Little, Brown.

Brown, Colin (1984) *Black and White Britain. The Third PSI Survey*. London: Heinemann.

147

Brown, Colin and **Gay, Pat.** (1985) *Racial Discrimination: 17 years after the Act.* London: Policy Studies Institute Report 646.

Bryce, James (1912) *South America: observations and impressions.* New York. Macmillan.

Bulmer, Martin (1980) On the feasibility of identifying 'race' and 'ethnicity' in censuses and surveys, *New Community* 8: 3-16.

Cashmore, E. Ellis (1984) *The Rastafarians.* London: Minority Rights Group Report 64.

Chiswick, Barry R. (1979) The economic progress of immigrants: some apparently universal patterns, in Fellner, William (ed.), *Contemporary Economic Problems 1979,* pp. 357-99. Washington: American Enterprise Institute.

Connor, Walker (1985) Who are the Mexican-Americans? A note on comparability, in Connor, Walker (ed.), *Mexican-Americans in Comparative Perspective,* pp. 2-28. Washington: The Urban Institute.

Daniel, W. W. (1968) *Racial Discrimination in England,* Harmondsworth: Penguin.

Davis, Allison, Gardner, Burleigh B., and **Gardner, Mary** (1941) *Deep South: a social anthropological study of caste and class.* Chicago: University of Chicago Press.

De Vos, George, *et al.,* (1983) *Japan's Minorities: Burakumin, Koreans, Ainu and Okinawans.* London: Minority Rights Group Report 3.

Ehn, Billy (1986) *Det otydliga kulturmötet. Om invandrare och svenskar på ett dagham.* Malmo: Liber Förlag.

Essien-Udom, E. V. (1962) *Black Nationalism: a Search for identity in America.* Chicago: University of Chicago Press.

Field, Simon (1984) *The Attitudes of Ethnic Minorities.* London: Home Office Research Study 80.

Field, Simon (1986) Trends in racial inequality, *Social Studies Review* 1: 29-34.

Fryer, Peter (1984) *Staying Power: the history of black people in Britain.* London: Pluto.

Gaskell, George, and **Smith, Patten.** (1981) 'Alienated' black youth: an investigation of 'conventional wisdom' explanations, *New Community* 9: 182-93.

Gaskell, George, and **Smith, Patten** (1984) Young blacks' hostility to the police: an investigation into its causes, *New Community.* 12: 66-74.

Helweg, Arthur H. (1979) *Sikhs in England: the development of a migrant community.* Delhi: Oxford University Press.

Homans, George Caspar (1950) *The Human Group*. London: Routledge.

Hughes, Everett C. and **Helen M.** (1952) *Where Peoples Meet: racial and ethnic frontiers*. Glencoe, Illinois: The Free Press.

Jackson, Harold (1984) *The Two Irelands: the double minority*. Minority Rights Group Report 2, rev. ed.

Johnson, R. W. (1977) *How Long Will South Africa Survive?* London: Macmillan.

Kettle, Martin, and **Hodges, Lucy** (1982) *Uprising! the police, the people and the riots in Britain's cities*. London: Pan.

Kuper, Leo (1960) The heightening of racial tension, *Race* 2: 24–32.

Kuper, Leo (1977) *The Pity of it All: polarization of racial and ethnic relations*. London: Duckworth.

Kuper, Leo (1981) *Genocide. Its political use in the twentieth century*. New Haven: Yale University Press.

Kuper, Leo (1982) *International Action Against Genocide*. London: Minority Rights Group Report 53.

Kuper, Leo (1985) *The Prevention of Genocide*. New Haven: Yale University Press.

Layton-Henry, Zig (1984) *The Politics of Race in Britain*. London: Allen and Unwin.

Lelyveld, Joseph (1986) *Move Your Shadow: South Africa, black and white*. London: Abacus edn 1987.

Lemarchand, Rene and **Martin, David** (1974) *Selective Genocide in Burundi*. London: Minority Rights Group Report 20.

Lorimer, Douglas A. (1978) *Colour, Class and the Victorians: English attitudes to the Negro in the mid-nineteenth century*. Leicester: Leicester University Press.

Mörner, Magnus (1967) *Race Mixture in the History of Latin America*. Boston: Little Brown.

Mourant, A. E. (1983) *Blood Relations: blood groups and anthropology*. Oxford: Oxford University Press.

Palley, Claire (1974) *Constitutional Law and Minorities*. London: Minority Rights Group Report 36.

Palley, Claire, *et al.* (1986) *Co-existence in Some Plural European Societies*. London: Minority Rights Group Report 72.

Rex, John (1982) West Indian and Asian youth, in Cashmore, Ernest, and Troyna, Barry (eds), *Black Youth in Crisis* pp. 53–71. London: Allen and Unwin.

Selvon, Samuel (1956) *The Lonely Londoners*. London: Wingate.

Sieghart, Paul (1986) *The Lawful Rights of Mankind*. Oxford: Oxford University Press.

149

Smith, David J. (1977) *Racial Disadvantage in Britain: the PEP Report.* Harmondsworth: Penguin.

Stymeist, David H. (1975) *Ethnics and Indians: social relationships in a northwestern Ontario town.* Toronto: Peter Martin Associates.

Sundkler, Bengt, G. M. (1961) *Bantu Prophets in South Africa,* 2nd edn. London: Oxford University Press (1st edn, 1948).

Swann, Michael (Lord) (1985) *Education for All: the Report of the Committee of Inquiry into the Education of Children from Ethnic Minority Groups.* London: HMSO, Cmnd. 9453.

Tajfel, Henri (1978) *The Social Psychology of Minorities.* London: Minority Rights Group Report 38.

Thornberry, Patrick (1987) *Minorities and Human Rights Law.* London: Minority Rights Group Report 73.

Tumin, Melvin, M., (1961) *Social Class and Social Change in Puerto Rico.* Princeton: Princeton University Press.

Visram, Rozina (1986) *Ayahs, Lascars and Princes: Indians in Britain 1700–1947.* London: Pluto.

Walvin, James (1971) *The Black Presence: a documentary history of the Negro in England.* London: Orbach and Chambers.

Watson, Graham (1970) *Passing for White: a study of racial assimilation in a South African school.* London: Tavistock.

Watson, James, (ed.) (1977) *Between Two Cultures: migrants and minorities in Britain.* Oxford: Blackwell.

Whitaker, Ben (ed.) (1983) *Teaching About Prejudice.* London: Minority Rights Group Report 59 (rev. 1985).

White, Robin M. (1979) What's in a name? Problems in official and legal uses of 'race', *New Community* 7: 333–49.

Wilson, Anne (1987) *Mixed Race Children: a study of identity.* London: Allen and Unwin.

Wilson, William Julius (1978) *The Declining Significance of Race: blacks and changing American institutions.* Chicago: University of Chicago Press.

Index